Momma Zen

Momma Zen

WALKING THE
CROOKED PATH
OF MOTHERHOOD

KAREN MAEZEN MILLER

TRUMPETER • *Boston* • 2007

Trumpeter Books
An imprint of
Shambhala Publications, Inc.
Horticultural Hall
300 Massachusetts Avenue
Boston, Massachusetts 02115
www.shambhala.com

14 13 12 11 10 9 8

Printed in the United States of America

♾ This edition is printed on acid-free paper that meets
the American National Standards Institute z39.48 Standard.
♻ This book is printed on 30% postconsumer recycled paper.
For more information please visit www.shambhala.com.
Distributed in the United States by Penguin Random House LLC
and in Canada by Random House of Canada Ltd

Designed by Lora Zorian

The Library of Congress catalogues the previous edition
of this book as follows:
Miller, Karen Maezen.
Momma Zen: walking the crooked path of motherhood/
Karen Maezen Miller.—1st ed.
p. cm.
ISBN 978-1-59030-296-5 (hardcover)
ISBN 978-1-59030-461-7 (paperback)
1. Motherhood—Religious aspects—Zen Buddhism.
2. Zen Buddhism. 3. Mothers—Religious life. I. Title.
BQ9286.7.M68M55 2006
294.3'4440852—dc22
2006000178

Dedicated to my mother,
to my daughter,
and to the teacher I found in between

CONTENTS

Contents

AUTHOR'S NOTE
What Is Zen?

> Obaku said, "I do not say that there is no Zen, but that there is no Zen teacher."
>
> —*Blue Cliff Record*, case 11

Zen this, Zen that. You can read a lot of things about Zen and none of them will be accurate. Even this.

I've just written an entire book about motherhood, yet when I have to write an introductory page or two about Zen, I stutter and gasp. When I told my Zen teacher how reluctant I was to write this part, he said something Zen-like. He said, "Keep it simple."

As for the word *zen,* it is a Japanese word for a Chinese word for a Sanskrit word that means meditation. In Zen practice, meditation is "the Way." Zen Buddhism, then, means "the Way of the Buddha." The Way of the Buddha is not secretive, exotic, or esoteric. It is not distant or dead. It is exactly what you see in the image of Buddha that still abounds today: a human being sitting still.

Zen practitioners do what Buddha did, sit quietly still, to see what Buddha saw—the truth of our existence—and thereby end confusion, discontent, pain, and suffering. It sounds simple, and it is. It is just not easy.

Zen originated in India with Buddha's successors. An Indian meditation master named Bodhidharma brought it to China in the sixth century. It took root in the Tang dynasty (618–907), a period now called the golden age of Zen. Many of the teaching stories, or koans, featured at the beginning of each chapter come from this era. These stories, or cases, recount spontaneous dialogues between students and enlightened masters. They were compiled during the Song dynasty (960–1279) into several written collections still used every day in classical Zen training.

In the twelfth century Zen was carried to Japan, where it was invigorated in the teaching of Dogen Zenji (1200–1253), whose penetrating words—vital and relevant—also appear at the beginning of many of the chapters you'll read here.

As I stumbled forward in the writing of this book, caught up in the personal and picayune details of baby care, I was continually amazed by the practical guidance in these ancient words. But let me save you a step. Do not attempt to understand or interpret them. Do not think about them at all.

Here in the West, and most certainly for me, Zen is real. But much of what you hear and see about Zen is not. I am alternately amused and annoyed by the proliferation of the term *Zen-like* to describe every kind of commodity, from furniture to fashion to face cream. Zen is not like anything else. Zen is the direct realization, the incomparable experience of *what is*. Zen is motherhood. And you already know that motherhood is not like anything else.

Zen is as alive as your hands holding this book, as vivid as your sight perceiving each word. Zen is your life, fully experienced. And yes, it is the Way of the Buddha.

PART ONE

Crooked Path

HOW DO YOU GO
STRAIGHT ON
A CROOKED PATH?

I

Other Mothers

OVERWHELMED AND UNCERTAIN—
THERE'S NO OTHER KIND

> At the moment of giving birth to a child, is the mother
> separate from the child? You should study not only that you
> become a mother when your child is born, but also that
> you become a child.
>
> —DOGEN ZENJI, *Mountains and Waters Sutra*

*T*his book took time. It took the first two years of my
daughter's life to arrive at the inspiration and motivation. It took another three years to write, in scattered, stolen
hours of solitude. It took countless episodes of confusion, mad-
ness and exasperation to realize what I knew and what I would
never know.

Just a few months after my daughter's birth, I saw another
new mother on the corner at the end of my block. We were
both in midstroll, at midmorning, with our bundled babies. We
recognized in each other's hollowed eyes and stringy hair the

secret sign of kindreds. *I haven't slept in a month or bathed in a week.* We walked together that day and many days after. Our daughters grew older and able and played together. We shared our never-ending doubts, our discoveries, our complaints, and our whispered heartaches. Underlying our friendship was the sense, the certain fear, that all around us were better mothers who were thin and groomed, confident and competent. These mothers had resolved all the questions about feeding and sleeping, poop and potty training, preschool and playmates, teething and talking, paper or plastic, that kept us forever unsteady. They had happy, textbook, gifted babies. These were mothers with a method. They were doing all the right things. They were on all the right waiting lists. They could shower, style their hair, and dress in their cute prepregnancy clothes every day before breakfast. They shaved their legs, and they had sex with their husbands. More than that, they *wanted* to have sex with their husbands.

They had birthed not just a child but a fully formed ideology of parenthood. It made things look easy, and it made things right.

We imagined legions of these supermothers, and we admired them from a distance. Yet privately we despised them. We had been blindsided by how difficult motherhood was. In our hushed confessions and brutal self-appraisals, we revealed how very different, diminished, and isolated we thought we were. We were the Other Mothers, whose daily blunders and emotional upheavals qualified us for charter admission into the Other Mothers Club. In reality, of course, there was no such club, just a couple of Keystone moms admitting truths in exchange for consolation and understanding. *I bribed her with Cheetos! I swatted her! He bit me! I don't even like her right now! I can't do this anymore! What have I gotten myself into? I want out!* What comfort there was in these admissions. And in the easy responses we gave to one another: *Of course. I know. I understand. Me too.*

These were reactions that we might not get from our own mothers or sisters and would simply not suffice from our husbands. Sincere and patient, our spouses tried to help us out—and in that gesture alone revealed that they could never really understand. Help was temporary. Advice was merely topical. We needed a close and constant source of solidarity.

Although I was a latecomer to this particular abyss, I had free-fallen before. Six years earlier, a sloppy heartbreak landed me at—of all the crazy places—a Zen Buddhist temple. In the silent stillness of these strange surroundings, I cried my eyes dry. Over more visits and with more meditation practice, I gradually wore out my restless and petty schemes, my frantic wishing, and my desperate daydreams of a life with a different ending. I learned to calm the mental conflagration consuming me. I stopped beating myself up. I stopped nearly everything. Sometimes I would even stop thinking. Seconds later I would start up again, but in the widening space between one blathering thought and the next, I found a pristine and beckoning peace from my pounding anxieties. I became a Zen Buddhist, a practice that again and again brought me back into full possession of my own life.

In the accidental good fortune that can rise up when you fall apart, I had wandered into one of the practice centers led by the late teacher Taizan Maezumi Roshi. This smiling man, slight, polite, and ever so subtle, was one of the colossal figures in twentieth-century Zen. He had arrived in Los Angeles in 1956 as one of the first Japanese teachers to bring Zen to the West. At the time I met him, he was living his last essential years as a seminal force in American Zen. He died in 1995.

Maezumi Roshi said many marvelous and inscrutable things,

but one I remember most vividly is "Your life is your practice." Like nearly everything I heard him say, I thought it meant something else. Something deep and beyond mere mortal comprehension. It does. But it also means just what it says. Your life is your practice. Your spiritual practice does not occur someplace other than in your life right now, and your life is nowhere other than where you are. You are looking for answers, insight, and wisdom that you already possess. Live the life in front of you, be the life you are, and see what you find out for yourself.

Easier said than done, I realize today, more than ten years after hearing those words for the first time. Understanding it or not, I did get on with life, laughter, love, work, matrimony, and the precipitous path of early motherhood. At this point, grasping for familiar ground, the words echoed back: Your life is your practice. *Oh, you mean this life?* This tripping up, breaking down, crying-out-loud life? This I'm-no-good-as-a-mother life? I turned the power of silent observation on the chaos within.

All of that grumbling about Other Mothers was what Zen calls "putting a head on your head," conjuring up comparisons, judgments, ruminations, and criticisms and, in the process, producing interminable suffering in my own mind. I was doing what we all do but precisely what I had been taught not to do. The events I describe in this book kept waking me up and making it clear. One head will do.

Motherhood is a spiritual practice. It is a crash course in wisdom. It is your spiritual legacy lying in wait for the taking. How else do you suppose mothers always end up knowing best? You do not have to mount a formal spiritual quest to uncover spiritual truths. I have, and it helps me. But you might not. As a mother, you have many priorities. Those priorities are nothing but your practice. If you allow it, being a mother is one of the most amazing, miraculous, mysterious, dignifying, and illuminating things you will ever do. However the experience unfolds for you, my aim is to help you cut through to the nub of it and appreciate things as they are.

There are books that tell you how to spiritualize your skills as a parent. There are books that instruct you about Buddhism and Zen, meditation and mindfulness. There are books that admonish you to be a better parent and thereby produce a better child. This is not one of those books, although it may inspire you to pursue all of those things. If so, you no doubt have the resources to find the information you need.

One day, in the thick of writing and rewriting this book, I plopped momentarily on the floor to play dolls with my four-year-old daughter. Then she said something. She said something innocent, startling, and wise, and I ran off to my computer to record it. She followed behind, disappointed, and I told her I had to write down what she had just said.

"Is that book about me?" she puzzled.

"Well, sort of," I waffled, to console her.

"It's not a book about motherhood!" she exclaimed, flush with the sudden thrill of discovery. "It's a book about childhood!"

She had beaten me, again, to the full understanding of Master Dogen's words about the oneness of mother and child, the understanding that upends the delusion of being separate and adversarial, the understanding that unlocks all the answers. The life of a mother is the life of a child: you are two blossoms on a single branch. It's only my egocentric point of view that is limited—the view that *I* am over here, and *she* is over there driving me crazy. To be a fuller, a more compassionate and even-minded mother, live as though there were no gap and become the child. *Yeah, right.* I promise you: there will be times when you see through the fog of your fears and fatigue and know exactly what I mean.

Your life as a mother will reveal self-evident insights. It will show you more clearly who you are and what life really is. It will prove how capable and creative you are, how boundless and free. You are just not likely to believe it right away. You will suspect that there's something you're not getting, something you're missing. You'll think you're not clever, good, or natural. This book aims to save you some of the savagery of your own self-criticism. It offers a tiny bit of help and a handful of advice, but mostly it gives a close and constant source of solidarity.

Stuck in stroller traffic, I came to suspect that we were all Other Mothers, or rather, that there was no *other* kind. A lifetime supply of insufficiency arrives with the stretch marks. Moments of self-assurance in motherhood do occur—joyful, satisfying, and complete—but they are just moments. In between are long, lonely spells when you feel lost and clueless. Ahead is another blind curve leading you somewhere you've never been. Yes, this crying-out-loud life *is* your crooked path, whose bumps and bends cannot be negotiated through mere reasoning. Time and again you'll be stripped of your preconceptions, judgments, ideas, theories, and opinions of motherhood and left to go straight on through the inexplicable experience itself. These gulfs of incomprehension bring the opportunity for spiritual growth and self-acceptance. It is an unexpected gift and not always recognized. That *you* recognize your gift is my aspiration with these recollections. These words thus flow from my heart to yours, from one other mother to one other mother or mother-to-be. I know. I understand. Me too.

2

Just Love

THE FIRST AND LAST WORD ON
THE SUBJECT OF MOTHERHOOD

> Even poor or suffering people raise their children with deep
> love. Their hearts cannot be understood by others. This can
> be known only when you become a father or a mother.
> They do not care whether they themselves are poor or rich;
> their only concern is that their children will grow up. They
> pay no attention to whether they themselves are cold or hot,
> but cover their children to protect them from the cold or
> shield them from the hot sun. This is extreme kindness. Only
> those who have aroused this mind can know it, and only
> those who practice this mind can understand it.
>
> —Dogen Zenji, "Instruction for the Tenzo"

It strikes me as best to begin with love. The word will never
again mean so much.

Of course you love your spouse. You love your parents and
brothers and sisters. You love your friends. You love your home

and perhaps your hometown. You love your dog. You may love your work. You might attest to loving your alma mater, mashed potatoes, or reading on a rainy day.

But *this* is love. The feeling you have for your child is so indescribably deep and consuming that it must qualify as one of the few transcendent experiences in your plain old ordinary life. It arrives spontaneously as though part of afterbirth. It is miraculous and supreme and irrevocable. It makes all things possible.

There is a certain attitude, perhaps unavoidable, that most of us seem to adopt as we grow up. It is a kind of self-satisfied conclusion that our parents didn't love us. Oh, they might have loved us, but they didn't love us *enough*. They didn't love us the right way. They didn't love us just so. Have your own child and you will penetrate into the utter absurdity of that idea. You will love your child as your parents loved you and their parents loved them. With a love that is humbling and uncontrived, immense and indestructible. Parents err, of course, and badly. They can be ignorant, foolish, mean, and far worse, in ways that you can come to forgive in them and try to prevent in yourself. But this wholesale shortage of parental love at the crux of everyone's story must be the product of shabby and self-serving recollections. Now that you are a mother, set that story aside, forgetting everything you thought you knew about love.

When my daughter was born, I saw my husband fall in love for the first time. He is a good and loyal man, and he loves me. But he has never lost his footing with me, not in the goofy, tumbledown way he surrendered on first sight to his baby girl.

Within days of bringing our tiny daughter home, my husband took dibs on the nighttime feedings. Born six weeks early, she had mastered bottle-feeding in the hospital but was weak and reluctant at the breast. There was a double bed crowded into our nursery, a relic of the room's recent use for guests, and there he slept, inches away from the mews, rasps, and mysterious *eap*s that emanated from her crib. He slept there eagerly and even well, waking every three hours to dispense her bottles. Although most nights I was waking too, like a shell-shocked soldier, to pump my raw and weeping breasts, the nights belonged to him.

So intense were his affections that I was jealous. Not jealous of him, jealous of *her*. He was hurrying home in the late afternoons to see *her*. Calling home hourly to check on *her*. Cradling *her* in the warm hollow of his chest for that last hour of sleep at dawn's early light. How could he possibly love an old, tired, slob of a frump like me anymore? I looked at my love-struck husband looking at her and raised an eyebrow.

I was all wound up and wrongheaded, and I hadn't yet realized that there was plenty of love to go around. Leave it to our cat to state the obvious. She was a whiny and temperamental thing, and we expected her to make trouble when the baby came home—jumping in the crib, taking wide swipes and big bites out of the unsuspecting adversary. I had searched the baby stores and the Internet for some kind of delicate-looking defense that I could install over the crib to keep our sweet kitty from eating the rival child. I'd draped a mosquito net over the bed to foil the attack. The cat knew better; the cat knew everything, and she recognized a good thing when she saw it. Within hours of our arrival from the hospital the cat was sitting peaceably as close to the three of us as she could get. Forever after, there would never be the slightest menace in her approach. The net over the crib would only ensnare dust. Our family was a love fount, and kitty was more than happy just to be in on the overflow.

In these early and unending days I was exhausted all of the time and depressed most of the time, but I came to a different and awed understanding of what life is. It's not what you think it is. First, what you call your life is not yours at all—not yours to plan, manipulate, or control, at least not very often. That's a staggering realization. I was humiliated to see that the maturity and serenity I thought I had achieved was simply the result of having things my way all the time. If life wasn't mine, what was it? In fleeting moments of deep satisfaction and insight, I saw the absolute truth of life: the unbroken line of love that had led to my existence and would lead on through my daughter. My mother's love, her mother's love, her mother's love, and back and back forever ago. Love that is no mere word, love that goes beyond feeling, love that is life itself. I was filled with a rush of respect for all mothers everywhere. *This* was how we all got here. What miracles, what sacrifice, what love! I never knew, nor could I have, before now. Can you imagine this love? Can you anticipate it, fabricate it, measure and evaluate it? No, you can't, you can only *be* love, and your child will release its magnitude within you.

Turns out you can take or leave the mashed potatoes.

No matter how miserable I was at the moment, I knew that life itself was overwhelmingly and infinitely good. This is the balm for all the bad days ahead. This is the only fix. This is the source and strength that lifts you up as you bottom out time and again.

Just love.

3

No Expectation

WHAT NOT TO EXPECT WHEN YOU'RE EXPECTING

Let go and make yourself independent and free, not being bound by things and not seeking to escape from things.

—Yuanwu

*T*he first signs that none of this would go according to plan appeared early on. Early, early on, if I'd been alert enough to weave the circumstances of my life into a coherent plotline. Would I ever have children? Would I ever even want them? My first marriage was childless by choice and extended into my midthirties. My second marriage was at midlife. By the time I was prepared to answer the second question, *Yes, I want a child,* the first question seemed to be answering itself, *No, you can't have one.* Without any apparent barrier, I simply could not get pregnant. I was too old, I told myself. I'd waited too long, and the choice was no longer mine. Case closed. I was furious at having lost the chance to have what I'd never even wanted.

And then, in a magic moment of old-fashioned fertility, I conceived. I was forty-two. Looking back, I saw that doing nothing to prevent pregnancy was not quite the same as doing something to get there. What I did was simply take my basal body temperature and have sex on cue, but even that required that I discard the ambivalence that I'd long carried about the issue. If it happens, it happens, I had been telling myself with a comfortable dose of confidence that it wouldn't.

So I was pregnant. I was going to have a baby girl. It wasn't difficult. I wasn't sick. Things rolled merrily along. I focused on how unchanged my life would be as a result of a child. The guest room would remain the guest room/study with its double bed, books, filing drawers, fax machine, and computer; we'd just put the crib in this little corner right here. Perfect fit. No problem. Of course I would still be working from home! Of course I would have time for this and that and everything. I would still be me, wouldn't I? I was intent on avoiding all the questions and clutter that I felt crowding in on my tidy little world. All those baby things! All that stuff! A crib *and* a bassinet? A car seat *and* a carrier? Surely I could do without. Babies, after all, could sleep in shoe boxes.

That they call this state "expecting" is one of many cruel paradoxes life has in store for a mother. Expecting what? A first-time mother has no idea what to expect from the experience, nor should she, but none of us let ourselves off that easily. We think we are supposed to *know* something and proceed to do it all the *right* way, thereby achieving the *best* outcome. What's so bad about that? you might ask. Nothing, by itself. The well-being of a pregnant mother and her child is a worthy goal, but examine just how much more than well-being you expect from your expectations: freedom from risk, trouble, surprises, and pain; adherence to your plan; ease and confidence; ecological correctness; intact execution of the approved color scheme; command control of the delivery; eradication of all doubts and fears; and a product that is judged by all objective standards to be a beautiful and brilliant child. Expectations accomplished, early admission, here we come!

By the end, you really will know something. You'll know that well-being is all that matters, and that you can handle even less than that.

Until then, you'll climb a craggy bluff of fear in your pregnancy and scale it in your own way. Where I sought to escape my fear, others arm themselves against it with information and ideology. They research methods and theories and gather advice and referrals. They collect the multitude of opinions that are lofted like arrows at their bull's-eye bellies. I was astonished when a friend announced, by way of a question, "You'll be using cloth diapers, won't you?" She had made up not only her mind but mine as well. It must be nice to have that sense of self-determination and control. Too bad it's only a sense.

In truth, I hadn't given thought to any of it. To believe that I could reason it out, to think that I could know for sure what was right or best, to presume that I was in charge, was already far beyond me. From its first bloated moment, pregnancy had seemed to me a lesson in losing it, a lesson in letting go. So it is. Can you imagine any other scenario in which you would pack on fifty extra pounds and never once pause to flick a speck of powdered sugar off your doughnut? Where you would fall so effortlessly, so helplessly to sleep before sunset? Where you would lose yourself in misty deliberations of lavenders, blues, and yellows; polka dots, pinks, and Poohs? Can you imagine a scenario in which an exquisitely miniature yet still massive head and all the rest actually emerges from your body? By hook or crook, it all comes down to letting go.

It's not a matter of expecting less or expecting more, expecting the best or expecting the worst. Expecting anything just gets in the way of the experience itself. And the experience itself is a stunner.

I can remember over the course of my pregnancy stark moments of full amazement at what I had *not done*. I had done nothing, and yet here it was: conception, gestation, and transformation of magnificent and unknowable proportions, all occurring outside the medium of thought and beyond my force of will. *This must be what they call creation.* It must be what I am.

And so I arrived at the place, late in the wait, when your ob-gyn or hospital invites you to complete a "birth plan." This is typically a simple one-page questionnaire about your preferences in labor, chiefly about dealing with pain. To be fair, this is a useful thing, especially for those of us who have not yet considered the distress and tedium of labor. I chuckled. This exercise reminded me of the common anxiety dream in which you're about to take a final exam for a course in which you never attended a class. Having never given birth, on what basis would I make a birth plan? How could I know now how my delivery would go? And what use is a plan at the bone-splitting moment of truth, especially what amounts to *last month's* plan?

I was skeptical, but I completed it dutifully. Then things started to go wrong.

At my seven-month prenatal visit, my blood pressure was slightly elevated. I also complained about swelling in my feet. True, that is common for midsummer pregnancies. Yet every day my discomfort grew. I could no longer sit in a chair without having my feet elevated. The first steps when getting out of bed were excruciating. Socks dug deep trenches in my ankles. I spent hours scanning the Internet for remedies and reassurances. Normal, normal, normal, I saw everywhere—indeed, it was what I wanted to see—but none of the fixes I tried made it one bit better.

My mother called with worries of her own. She had been dropping weight all year long with a diligent diet, but nothing seemed to reduce the size of her belly. It was getting bigger. Thrilled with my late-life pregnancy and a bonus round of grandmotherhood, she herself had begun to feel and look pregnant, she said. A series of unhurried examinations through the HMO referral system had finally landed her in the hands of an expert. He warned her of the worst it could be: ovarian cancer, with its subtle warning signs of abdominal swelling and vague pain. Surgery was scheduled within a week. At the very best, she would miss the trip to the West Coast for her grandchild's homecoming. The very worst was unthinkable.

I stopped thinking, or trying to wear shoes. I closed my eyes and shut my ears and, concerned only about the circumference of my thighs, stepped on the scales. Twelve pounds in less than two weeks. My sister called with the surgeon's report. Mom had stage IV ovarian cancer, the most advanced, and it had spread throughout her abdominal cavity. All kinds of body parts came out during surgery, and those left would be taken later, although we didn't believe it then, blitzing past the plainspoken prognosis to grab onto the tiny odds of her recovery, 5 percent, which suddenly sounded so feasible. Mom had always finished in the top 5 percent of everything.

At my own doctor's office the next day, my weight, urine, and blood pressure spelled out something obvious. "I don't feel well," I said woefully. "You have preeclampsia," the doctor said. This was the word that I had been browsing past all summer on the Web. Preeclampsia is never neatly defined because it is still so poorly understood. For unknown reasons, preeclampsia favors first-time mothers—first-time older mothers even more so. They develop hypertension and protein in the urine and experience swelling, headaches, and blurred vision. The symptoms point the way to grave and even fatal consequences to the untreated sufferer: liver or kidney damage, convulsions, and coma. Deliver the child and preeclampsia goes away.

I liked my doctor for plenty of reasons. She was smart and fast, a pedigreed practitioner in a shorts-and-sandals suburb. In her quiet efficiency I found everything I needed to confer guru status. She was cheery, matter-of-fact, and completely noninvasive during the first six months of pregnancy. I interpreted her inaction as reverence for the mystery of birth. That made me unafraid. But this time was different. I had preeclampsia. I was instantly and totally petrified.

The doctor stood staring down my disbelief and spoke with unartful clarity. *Go check into the hospital. Do not go home. You may last until the weekend.* If she could lower my blood pressure with bed rest, she hoped to gain a few vital days of gestation. Each day between now and then would help the baby's lungs develop. I was thirty-three weeks into the forty weeks of a full term. Lungs are developed by thirty-four weeks.

There was good luck in this, although not the kind of luck you'd wish for. Preeclampsia can develop earlier in the second trimester, and mothers are hobbled at home or in the hospital until the odds for the baby's survival tip in favor of early birth— even a critically premature one. Because preeclampsia had occurred late in my pregnancy, the baby was certainly better off outside my womb than inside, where, stressed and failing, the placenta was nourishing her less and less.

But I didn't buy it. I couldn't buy it. This was going to go my way, I willed, this was going to go the distance. Stocked with relaxation tapes and a meditator's self-assurance, I coasted through the next week in the hospital. My blood pressure stabilized, my urine normalized, and the swelling went down. My performance convinced some of the nurses. "There's nothing wrong with you," one uttered under her breath in that nurses-know-best tone as she took my blood pressure for the umpteenth time. My doctor reluctantly let me go home. "I've never seen this work before," she warned. "Now you know what is possible," I preached, thinking I had prevailed.

Two days later I was back at the doctor's, my blood pressure soaring. An ultrasound found that even as I had reveled in victory over my imagined foe, my daughter had lost half a pound during my week of bed rest, and she had no pounds to spare. I thought I had won, but she had, in fact, lost, as she would every time I mistook my own fears and desires for what was best. It was impossible to believe, but this part of my job was over. Pregnancy had prepared me as I hoped my mother's life had prepared her. It was time to let go. It would always be time to let go.

4

Being Unprepared

NOW DELIVERING THE UNPLANNED
PORTION OF YOUR LIFE

Sekiso Osho asked, "How can you proceed on further from the top of a hundred-foot pole?" Another eminent teacher of old said, "You, who sit on the top of a hundred-foot pole, although you have entered the Way you are not yet genuine. Proceed on from the top of the pole, and you will show your whole body in the ten directions."

—*Gateless Gate*, case 46

So much of pregnancy seems to be a preparation—literally and figuratively: The physical changes—first subtle, then gargantuan—as one body recasts itself as two. The mental and emotional transit from shock to acceptance and excitement. The momentum of getting everything ready—the house, the room, the walls, the closet and drawers, the crib and clothes. All the imaginary trips you'll take anticipating the unimaginable experience of childbirth.

You'll do them, yes, replaying timeless rituals of the maternal. But do not expect to be prepared. Life is preparing you to be unprepared. To step from the top of a hundred-foot pole. To have no idea what will happen next. To do whatever is required, without judgment or hesitation. To trust events as they unfold, and to trust the host of people, many of them strangers, who will arrive just in time to guide and help you.

There is a ride at Disneyland called Peter Pan's Flight. It is one of the original rides in the park, so it lacks the pomp and flourish of what the corporate folks now call "imagineering." Growing up in southern California, my sisters and I were frequent riders on Peter Pan's Flight, and we remember it still. More precisely, we remember nothing of the ride but everything about the way it begins.

Crammed into a little two-seater of a make-believe ship, you creak and lurch forward into the pitch blackness of the adventure ahead. As you ratchet around a turn and leave daylight behind, the tinny voice of Pan trails, "C'mon everybody, here we gooooooooo!"

That's what giving birth is like. That tells you nothing; that tells you everything. That's my point.

There are cataclysmic moments in life when you realize its perpetual motion, when you experience for yourself the awesome rush of the scientific fact that there is no such thing as solid ground. Car accidents are one. Combat is probably another. And childbirth.

In actuality, there is never any such thing as solid ground, but strapped securely inside our heads, where we live most of the time, things seem pretty predictable and safe. We think we are the captain of the ship. We are prepared to steer, to give orders, and to reach our intended destination just the way we want to. How we fear our navigational errors! How earnestly we aim! When you go into labor, you see that you are not the captain of the ship. You are the ship. There is no captain. There are only the waves.

The morning after my last doctor's visit, I reported to the delivery room for my little hurry-up baby to be born. You might expect that a dire situation would require dire intervention, such as an emergency C-section. My doctor advised me that in situations of distress such as mine, a vaginal birth was actually less traumatic for both the mother and baby. Labor would be induced. An epidural would be required to reduce the pain because pain would further elevate my dangerously high blood pressure. I did not object.

The monitors and cuff were strapped on. The IV drips were started. The pellets of whatever magic potion was supposed to soften my cervix were inserted. Then, nothing happened. Nothing happened all morning. My husband and I read the paper. We made phone calls. He went to Starbucks. Nothing happened all afternoon. We watched Montel Williams. Then Peter Jennings. The doctor came by to tell us nothing was going to happen until the next day at best, so we should go to sleep and start all over again in the morning.

I've slept before in hospitals, but I don't remember how. On this night, with a fetal heart monitor around my bulging gut, a blood pressure monitor automatically inflating every half minute around my arm, and a magnesium sulfate drip to prevent a seizure, sleep would elude me. I was crimped and stiff from long days of bed rest. My pounding blood pressure, I realize now, had given me a horrific neck ache. If the ache had been inches higher in my head, it would have signaled an imminent seizure. As it stood now, nothing was imminent but waiting. Alone in my suffering, I wanted desperately to get ahead, get around, get through, or otherwise fast-forward to a favorable outcome. I could do none of that. All I had to work with was my mind. I could lose it or I could use it.

Focus on what is in front of you; my Zen teacher's words rang through my head. I opened my eyes in the darkened room and, from my supine position on the bed, saw what was in front of me: the round, high-beam surgical light recessed into the ceiling above. I focused on it, breathing in, breathing out. Soon I recognized its shadowy shape as symbolic of the sun. Breathing in, breathing out. The sun was now dark. Breathing in, breathing out. Soon it would rise. Breathing in, breathing out. Inching above the horizon, it would gradually become blazingly open and full. Breathing in, breathing out. *Open,* I repeated to myself, breathing in, breathing out.

I nudged my drowsing husband in the chair next to me. "When the sun comes up, everything will be okay!" I declared with urgent certainty. He went back to sleep.

I don't know how these instructions occurred to me. When you, too, focus your concentration and quiet your mind, intuitive knowing arrives. Months later, after I sheepishly told this story, a Zen friend exclaimed, "Oh, Maezumi Roshi gave you the meditation on the rising sun. He gave all pregnant women the meditation on the rising sun!" By this point, Roshi had been dead for four years.

I focused on the light all that night as the pains began. I focused on the nurse as the day shift arrived. I focused on the wetness when my water soon broke. I focused on the needle when the anesthesiologist hurried in. I focused on my doctor when she returned, summoned for the unexpectedly sudden delivery. I focused on my breath. I focused on the counting. I focused on the push.

My daughter was born, her lungs just ready, with a magnificent roar. Another on-time, unplanned arrival. The whole body was revealed in the ten directions.

Where once, in recent history and ancient practices, families of women surrounded women at this hour, now so many of us have so few. My mother was three states away, only days home from unplanned surgery, my sisters with her, the moment my daughter was born. I called her, giddy with relief and joy, from the delivery room. We laughed and cried at the aching contradiction of the moment: my four-pound daughter born, strong and well, my mother almost certainly on her way to dying. And both truths beyond prediction or belief only weeks before.

Preeclampsia disappears upon delivery. Or so they say. Mine overstayed, a stubborn guest. My daughter and husband were hustled off to the neonatal intensive care nursery, the NICU, while I was reinstated in the high-risk unit, on more magnesium to prevent convulsions. The trip to the nursery was deemed too risky for a new mother with a systolic blood pressure over 150. I stayed bed-bound for two days while the nurses conspired to bend the rules. My husband brought me Polaroid photos of our blanketed girl in her own Isolette adorned with a handwritten pink placard: Georgia Grace. The neonatal nurses must vie for the high honor of the task—to decorate these courageous little soldiers with the careful pen strokes of a name.

When I looked at the fuzzy photos of my daughter, and later, when I wheeled into the NICU for my first visit, she looked like a bug. Someone else's bug. I didn't know her as my own. It was a shock, meeting the stranger that I would love and live with for the rest of my life. I didn't recognize her! She was minuscule by any standards but the NICU's, where her weight and hardiness had already graduated her to the upper ranks. Cradling her in the crook of my arm, just sixteen inches tip to toe, I knew two things. She was fine. And she was in the very best place she could be.

So was I. I had time to make calls and write lists, marshal my friends to take care of everything. I had no nursery yet, just a crib. My best friend flew in from Texas and in two days finished the task with an outfitter's flourish. And then the gifts came. From friends, neighbors, and family, and many more from people I didn't know. Touched by her sad illness, my mother's friends rushed in to uplift her in the only way available to them. By helping me. Packages arrived by the dozens, with clothes, blankets, toys, books, and the bitsy preemie things that were never on the list. In these kindnesses, I saw how compelling our need must be to connect to other lives. I felt the sheltering generosity inherent in the ritual of the "shower." I believed that each gift delivered compounded quantities of love and hope. I would withhold none of these things from me or from my baby. To accept any gift wholeheartedly, I came to realize, was to accept life, and everything in it, as our own.

The world had stepped forward to welcome her. When my daughter came home, nearly two weeks later, there was not one thing lacking in our preparation. The plan was kaput, but the unplanning was perfect. You could call it all misfortune, or you could call it luck. You could call it sad, or you could call it happy. The point is, I could handle it. We can handle anything when we exchange our worries and fears for alertness and spontaneity, when we focus solely on what is in front of us, and when we leap into the sheer wonder of the unplanned life.

5

Life Force

NOTHING LITTLE ABOUT IT

In spring wind
peach blossoms
begin to come apart.
Doubts do not grow
branches and leaves.

—Dogen Zenji, "Viewing Peach Blossoms
and Realizing the Way"

I no longer had any reason not to be ready, but still—how can you feel ready for this? My doctor warned me that my baby might not be discharged for six weeks or so, the time that she would otherwise have spent gestating. Yes, that meant hard days at the hospital, anxious setbacks, and desperate yearnings, but it made such reasonable, comfortable sense. Let her stay in the nimble hands of the sturdy nurses. Leave on those wires, tubes, and sensors, her lifeline to fail-proof medical salvation. What's the rush?

I began to relax into a long wait, easing into a routine made easier by its guarantee that my daughter's life depended on someone other than me. They called on her twelfth day, the morning after the monitor showed that her heart pumped in perfect tempo all through the night. *Home today? Why not at least one more night of perfect heartbeats?*

They must be nuts.

I suspect all new parents feel the same, wheeled out onto the hospital curb after one or two nights. *Here's that new life you ordered. Now get on with it!*

Infant in arms, you teeter forward, feebly aware that you have just passed to the far side of time. Whatever your age—and mine was irretrievably ancient—this first move-out, take-home day of motherhood is a demarcation. You have reached a summit of sorts in the story of your life. However long and spectacular a slope it proves to be, it is nonetheless downhill from here on out. The leaf turns, the blossom fades, new branches grow, and buds spring forth. Life's incessant rhythm, its eternal pattern, has been fulfilled.

Our bud was tipping the scales at four pounds, three ounces. Do you know how much of nothing that is? How colossal our doubts? How infinite our fears? Taken by itself, just the fear of dropping her could freeze me in stasis until the end of time. Of course, time wasn't something that I had time for anymore.

We careened to the hospital, adrenalized by the significance of the mission. Once there we lingered and looked about. Wasn't somebody going to give us something? A test, a handout, a checklist? Go ahead and take her, everyone urged, with nothing more than a smile. *We need supervision! We're not qualified!* We begged a remedial lesson in how to fold a blanket; we settled for oral instructions in giving a bath. *You actually pick her up and put her in the water?* My husband and I looked at each other in wordless accord: this child would not be getting any baths in the foreseeable future.

The two-week hiatus had been a hellish disruption, true, but it had neatly shielded us from the shock that slaps all new parents after delivery, the shock that comes with the words "Here's your baby." Dazed on the sidelines, VIP visitors in the intensive-care nursery, we had kept a respectful distance from the expert interventions. From the buffer zone, we had mistaken our daughter's life for the scribbling on a chart and the cadence of a monitor. Georgia's life wasn't a measurement, it now dawned on us. Georgia's life was—gasp—*ours.*

I fumbled her into her going-home clothes, a preemie size 0 and still two sizes too big. I struggled with the Barbie-sized booties. Like everything I was about to do for the next gazillion days, baby wardrobing was sheer guesswork. I had brought one of those teeny skullcaps that come with every ensemble, assuming by their omnipresence that no newborn should ever be without one. Looking on, the neonatologist grinned.

"It must be a hundred degrees outside," she smiled on this late summer day. "She won't need that."

I look at the picture my husband snapped then, me in the standard-issue wheelchair, ghostly eyes and ashen skin, cradling my swaddled cargo. I wear my freshly cut and blow-dried hair like a funny hat. It was such a misspent effort to pull myself together. Overwhelmed by the events, I'd hurried straight to the hair salon in the first days of recuperation to restore my trusty self-image. The treatment didn't quite take. Under the hair I looked so old, so tired, and so scared.

"Don't worry," the doctor said, reading my fretful mind. "She's strong and full of life. You have a greater chance of keeling over dead than she does." There was no morbidity in her words, just the obvious truth. My daughter's life was new and pure and immeasurably potent. Mine was, by any reasonable estimate, half spent. The doctor was reassuring me that my daughter wasn't sick. She wouldn't break. There was such a thing as life force, and by God, she had it. My life force? I must say it was radically and irreparably altered.

Two months later at our Buddhist baby blessing, my teacher would bring up the same point, sharing the startling sentiment in this story called "Real Prosperity" from *Zen Flesh, Zen Bones.*

A rich man asked Sengai to write something for the continued prosperity of his family so that it might be treasured from generation to generation.

Sengai obtained a large piece of paper and wrote: "Father dies, son dies, grandson dies."

The rich man became angry. "I asked you to write something for the happiness of my family! Why do you make such a joke as this?"

"No joke is intended," explained Sengai. "If before you yourself die your son should die, this would grieve you greatly. If your grandson should pass away before your son, both of you would be broken-hearted. If your family, generation after generation, passes away in the order I have named, it will be the natural course of life. I call this real prosperity."

We give our children life. How, then, can we expect to keep our own intact afterward? But we do. We haven't yet recognized our new position in the natural order of things, and we keep trying to return to where we were before. At first, out of innocence: *Let me get back my looks. Let me get back my energy. Let me get back into the swing of things.* Then with ferocious will: *Let me get back to my own life!* So goes the battle between the old and the new, the giver and the taker, the parent and the child.

I am talking about something more than just the gauzy cycle of life. Sure, you're older now and one day you're going to die, but before that, you have to *die.* Your child has arrived and the battle has been joined. It is the battle to the death of your ego. The demise of your selfishness and impatience. The end of your idle distractions and carelessness. The decline and fall of Numero Uno. Or so you must pray, because in this contest, you must lose and lose quickly. Pray that you will never bear the shattered consequences of winning when your child's safety, trust, and happiness are the casualties.

You have a greater chance of keeling over dead than she does.

Oh, if I had grasped the subtle wisdom being expressed in the doctor's benediction, I could have gone so much more gently into the coming days and nights.

We squinted into the sun on the long road home. She was my life. Her life was mine.

PART TWO

Losing Ground

DWELLING NOWHERE,
RAISE THE MIND

6

Sing Song

WHERE LULLABIES COME FROM

Streams and birds
Trees and woods
All recite
The name of the Buddha

—*Amitabha Sutra*

*I*n the house of a newborn, there are no walls. No doors, no clocks, no meals, no chores, no day, no night, none of the familiar coordinates we use to navigate our lives. We bring our babies home, and then the floor gives way and the roof collapses. Adrift in disorientation, I began to sing.

I remember the first time. Shortly after sunrise, in my robe and slippers, I carried my just-fed daughter out to the ponds and pines in our backyard. I held her and gazed at her perfect sleeping face, but there was another part of her I wanted to reach. *What do I do and how can I say?* I started to sing with the wind and birds. I sang the ABCs. It was the only children's song that I remembered.

How silly. It would be nearly a year before a word emerged from her lips, two years before she commanded language, and longer before she sounded the alphabet. ("Momma, what letter is ellemeno?") Still, I kept singing. I would sing as I fed and rocked and strolled with her. I sang as I changed a diaper. I made up songs and rhymes, short riffs that I would repeat in a continuous loop, until the singing and the doing were inseparable. The rocking song. The walking song. The bath song. I could say they were for her, and yet I knew the solace was for me. I was singing for her and for me without distinguishing the two.

Singing was not something that I was otherwise prone to. I'm not about to do anything that I'm not "good" at, and no one had asked me to sing since third-grade choir. This new singing was a kind of mindless chirping sprung from—where exactly? It was sometime later that I recognized singing as the entry point to pure being, an utterly empty, nonthinking state of mind that is the ultimate coping strategy. Every moment I was humming along, letting the music and words tumble out, was a moment I wasn't thinking dreary thoughts. I wasn't thinking anything at all.

Singing also activates another overlooked coping strategy: breathing. Singing *is* breathing, and breathing is life. Everything about the mystery of life is contained in breathing, and although we can do it without prompting, we usually stagger about, strangled by entangling thoughts, rarely breathing fully and sometimes forgetting to breathe at all. Deliver yourself to a doctor and she will listen to your chest and instruct you to breathe. Deliver yourself to an exercise guru and he will command you through paces while reminding you to breathe. Deliver yourself to a meditation teacher and she will show you how to sit still and breathe. Deliver a baby from your body and give a teensy nudge for the thrilling vibrato to commence. Do you want to have a deeper and fuller encounter with life? Have a deeper and fuller encounter with oxygen.

Singing is chanting, and chanting, too, is meditation. Don't presume there to be any difference between monks in the Middle Ages crooning into the hollow of their sanctuary and you in a raggedy bathrobe serenading from a rocking chair. This is your new spiritual practice: "Polly Wolly Doodle." How brilliant, how superb that nature evokes in mothers this predilection for song!

Consider the lullabies, the ones you will make up and all the famous ones that you can stitch together in remnants of remembered lyrics and melodies. How deep and true the calling in these songs! They are such gentle dirges for the doneness of the day. Each beckons to relax and relinquish, to fall into the emptiness of sleep. Every time I sang a lullaby, I realized the invitation was for me. Could I give up the day? Could I empty myself and have no more second thoughts or worries? Could I accept each day as whole and complete even if not one thing was accomplished to my satisfaction? Or did I expect that my daughter would drift into repose while I churned and fretted, preoccupied and impatient? This was my lesson in the lullaby, and I was not so quick a study. Luckily, each day brought another night's practice. When I heard other mothers lament that their babies never napped, or fought against bedtime, I sympathized with the babies. Giving up is not so easy to do. Try it yourself. The songs will show you how.

My own mother was chasing the sleep that had once been so effortless for her. Perhaps because of the hard certainty of her illness, perhaps because of the chemistry of the cure, she had stopped sleeping. I sent her a copy of my favorite CD of children's lullabies, classical instrumentals that provided especially calm company. She played it for herself; I played it for myself; the music carried across the miles and mountains between us, she in her rocker, I in mine, on either end of this thin, thin, eternal filament called life. The music helped us cry, and then it helped us stop.

It so happened that the baby's room was stocked with a connoisseur's collection of classical music, because my daughter was born in the midst of a movement to engineer baby geniuses by playing Mozart's music in the nursery. (More than that, in utero.) Many well-intentioned gifts ensued. I can attest to the utter failure of the method. Beautiful music is heavenly, I agree, but I could hardly bear the intrusion, the imposition of yet one more thing to do the *right* way for the sake of my own ambition. No, she would hear a universe of sound and music and have to learn algebra the hard way.

Imagine how priceless our discovery when we took our first family vacation to the beach and watched our nine-month-old fall into bottomless slumber to the endless rhythm of the surf. We wore out three CDs and two boom boxes playing ocean recordings (no whales, no seagulls) throughout every nap and night for the next four years.

I, too, needed the soothing of a primordial tune. Songs bubbling up from my own depths with no sense or meaning. Songs from nowhere, with no end. Don't get me wrong: recorded music is nice. It can be comforting and enjoyable. But *made* music is magic. It occupies and transforms you; it becomes you.

Locked inside your house with only an infant as company, it is so easy to retreat still further into the confines of your mind. Your head will fill with the constant rat-tat-tat of worries, critiques, and woes. For the sound of company, you might take refuge in the telephone or the television, but what kind of company is that? Turn off the inner chatter, turn off the outer prattle, and you will realize that all of life has a hum and a rhythm, every sound is a song: the birds and bugs, the garbage truck, the wind and trees, the throttling jet, your breathing baby. It is the song of life. But you? No, you can't sing.

I once shared my singing tip with another mother. She waved me off with, "Oh, I don't sing." Precisely! Sing because you think you can't, because you don't know where the melody will go or what nonsense you'll invent. Stop thinking about what you can't do! Sing *as if* you could, and lose yourself and your cynicism in the song.

Later, when I began to read books to my daughter (you'll be surprised how soon you are inclined to begin), I sang the words on the page. It seemed too strange to announce the text straight on like some kind of foreign-language newscaster. Singing books was my habit until she looked up at me, at age two and a half, and said kindly, "No, Momma. Say it."

Made-up songs and music were the constant of our communication. They were acclimating me to the simpler rhythms of motherhood and opening my mind and heart to living spontaneously. Perhaps this is why mothers sing. By all means, sing. I sang my songs again and again until a long time later I realized I had forgotten the words. By then, *she* began singing.

7

Small Failures

THERE ARE NO MISTAKES, EVEN
THE UNFORGIVABLE ONES

My life is one continuous mistake.

—Dogen Zenji

*T*he first months were full of small failures, countless ways to fall short of measuring up.

I vastly overestimated my strength and her weakness. I failed to rest, never napped, and got sick. I was paranoid that I would infect her. I kept latex gloves and surgical masks in supply. On day three I called the hospital nursery in a panic. "I have a cold, what should I do?" Once they realized the risk I posed, they'd surely have me bring her back to the hospital for safekeeping.

"Wash your hands," came the reply. *Take care of yourself.*

Exhaustion made me brittle. A silent rage billowed and foamed against the sudden loss of everything mine—my body, my time, my space, and my life. In one of the raw utterances we tolerate from the terminally ill, my mother told me, "I wasn't surprised you never had children. I didn't think you had the temperament." She was right. Motherhood could be an unflattering mirror, and I resolved every day to try harder and be softer. *Be kind to yourself and others.*

I needed more help but was slow to see it and ashamed to ask. Mothers everywhere through all of time had done what I now seemed incapable of doing on my own. Ah, yes, but they were normal, and the evidence was mounting that I was seriously below average. Eventually I opened the door to other, loving hands. But it was never a mere request; it was a weighty admission. Much joy was lost in the time it took to shirk the guilt. *Get help, and ask for more.*

And I failed at breast-feeding. This was no small failure.

If I were building a case in my defense—and I would for the rest of my days—it would go like this: She was born six weeks before she had either the instinct or the strength for sucking. I sought counsel and training. I pumped myself six times a day to maintain my supply. I tried. We both tried. She was so small. I was desperate for her to eat anything. At best, I could supplement her formula feedings. By the time she was two months old, she still could not fill herself at the breast before collapsing within seconds into slack-jawed sleep. When colic set in, I stopped feeding her my milk until I rebuilt my diet, one bland food at a time. When that didn't work, I did it again.

I knew the benefits. I knew the medical preference. "How long should I go on trying?" I asked the pediatrician, begging an out. "Do not let this come between you and your baby," she said. She would not press me; she would not judge. She saw what I was too self-absorbed to realize yet: it was about the feeding, not the breast; it was about the baby, not me.

I called my mom. She told me her story. After nursing my older sister and me, she had my baby sister, who was born two weeks early. "I brought her home and tried for one day. It was nothing like the first two. I sent your dad out for bottles that night." No morning-after mourning for her. She pleaded with me, as any mother to a tormented child, "Don't be so hard on yourself."

We make a life of this: this falling short, this striking out. Rather, we make a life *story* out of this, because whose life isn't made up of melodramatic episodes of dashed hopes and disappointments, misfortunes and mistakes? Certainly, all manner of events transpire in life, but where exactly does this thing called a *mistake* take place? Only in our mind—our judging, critical, labeling mind. The mind that provides the nonstop narrative to our lives: "There you go again. Can't get it right. You'll never do it. Big mistake."

Buddhism teaches that all of life and all existences are perfect as they are. I can easily accept that about a bird or a fish or a rock, but hardly about my fellow human beings and never about me, a lowly bottle-feeding mother. You can substitute the circumstances in your own story (you know it by heart), and the comparisons and recriminations remain. How many of your thoughts are about not being good enough? My guess is nearly all of them. And none of them are the means for getting on with your life. They are the means for avoiding your life—detouring from what is right in front of you to make endless mental laps around the ground long ago covered and gone.

What would happen if the nit-picking narration were absent? What happens when you watch a TV football game with the sound turned off? The players still scramble, they still fall, but they are saved the injury of evaluation. The same would be true of your life. What is a mistake without the self-critical label? It is just what it is. It is always perfection in action—not perfect as in *better than something else* but perfect as in *complete*. Your actions need nothing—not analyzing, not punishment, not instant re-play. It is impossible not to do your best, you just don't *think* it's your best.

Yet Dogen calls his life "one continuous mistake." When the play-by-play goes quiet in a still and empty mind, a mistake is no different from no-mistake. It is just life, alert, awake, whole-hearted, unburdened, moment after moment, emancipated from right and wrong, continuously *as it is.*

Maezumi Roshi used to say, "I still have troubles. They're just not a problem."

Soon I gave up breast-feeding. There were no more prob-lems, except the doubts. I second-guessed every runny nose and infection. *What if?* I second-guessed her language development, her emotional security, and her still-untested IQ. I second-guessed my will, my stamina, and my instincts. Long after quit-ting breast-feeding, I am still nursing my starving ego. But I must stop. It only hurts me and, in turn, her. This is the most important object of this lesson. Practice acceptance on yourself so you can be kinder with your child. Practice nonjudgmental awareness of your life so you can save your loved ones from the cruelty of your own impossible standards and your hard-hearted disappointment. Practice greater faith and lesser blame. Take this blink of time when you are still stumbling at the gate, still awk-ward at the tasks, to turn down the sound and tumble freely in a state of grace.

Life is full of fits and starts. Some things are easy; some are not. Some things go and some things stop. Do your work; then set it down. There are no failures. *Forgive and forget yourself.*

8

Night Watch

A MEDITATION ON SLEEPLESSNESS

Within light there is darkness, but do not try to understand
 that darkness.
Within darkness there is light, but do not look for that light.
Light and darkness are a pair like the foot before and the foot
 behind in walking.

—Sekito Kisen, "The Identity of Relative and Absolute"

I could have endured all of this, and still more. I could have
plodded on through the zombie days. I could have rolled
with the punches and blown with the breeze. I could have mastered the moves and gotten good at it, but in all the commotion,
we suffered one last catastrophe—a home invasion.

A thief came in the darkness, into our private sanctuary, into
our haven of rest and nest of dreams, and stole the night.

My pregnancy guidebooks didn't have a chapter on this. The
doctor didn't bring it up. None of the well-meaning relatives and
neighbors, none of the Good Samaritans and gift givers, no
nurse, no friend, no stranger, no one ever took me aside in lov-

ing confidence and comradeship and whispered a word of the truth. So here it is, for your sake.

When you have a baby, the boundaries of a day are not boundaries at all. What you thought was a day—daylight followed by an evening meal and assorted frivolities—is only one-half of the day. A true day goes on much longer! A true day is a night and a day and a night again. A true day never ends. And you will be awake to see it, because sleep is not a given, it is not a law, it is not yours.

There.

So you lose a good bit of your precious sleep. But the most devastating loss is not the loss of sleep, it is the loss of what you thought was *yours*.

What's the big deal, you might wonder, in a world that treats sleep deprivation like a sport. Who isn't sleep deprived? I, too, had insomnia in pitiful little fits before motherhood. After one breakup I forgot how to sleep for nearly three months. I was seriously sleep disordered, but the disorder was *mine*, and I put up the good fight before letting it go.

Sleep is one of our most intractable attachments. We claw and clutch and crave it. We adorn and worship it. We four-hundred-thread count it. It is our one sovereign domain. We hide out there; we fantasize and burrow there; we think we can't live without it. You will see that you can live without it— just enough.

Between a mother and a child, sleeplessness unfurls like a torture device. Who will crack? Who will break? Blessedly, you will. You will give up and go forth to the cries. You will let go of your resistance, your willful inertia. You will drop the dead weight of your needs so you can gather up your child to feed, succor, and sleep. You will break with your greedy, sleepy, clandestine self. Yes, you will do it every time. This is your new spiritual practice:

waking up and getting out of bed. Over many nights of practice flinging back the covers and tearing loose from your attachment, deep wisdom will emerge. Everything, it seems, comes out of the night, and you are now its most alert and dependable eyewitness.

You are a witness to biology. The first months are the most simple to explain and the most difficult to endure. Sleep in newborns is a function of the stomach. Fill the stomach and sleep comes. Empty the stomach and sleep goes. It is not a matter, yet, of anything that anyone can convince you that you have mismanaged. But you will scarcely sleep in between. It is important that you place no more expectations on yourself during this period than the world expects of you. And the world expects nothing of you except to stay home, feed your child, and steal whatever sleep you can.

You will make it; you will make it to that one day soon when your child grows past the digestive tipping point and can consume enough to occupy his body for a full seven hours. This seven hours—this Magnificent Seven—is called "sleeping through the night." It is only *called* sleeping through the night, because to the parent of any one-, two-, three-, four-, or five-year-old, sleeping through the night is something that you say with great frequency but that occurs only intermittently. Everything comes out of the night, and you are the eyewitness.

You are a witness to neurology. At about eight months, the nature of sleep in your child will change. The center of sleep somehow shifts from the stomach to the brain, and your baby now sleeps in patterns just like you do: off to sleep, then—*hello!*—awake; off to sleep, then awake again. With our daughter, this was a period that found us latched to our computers, searching madly and suckered hopelessly into every come-on guaranteed to put a kid to sleep and keep her there: videos, CDs, books, creams, lotions, teddy bears, teas, and aromatherapies. We let all of these hucksters accuse us, and we paid their price, believing that we had somehow failed to properly train our child to sleep without waking.

You will make it; you will make it to that one day soon when your child stirs and turns and gently puts himself back to sleep. But there will be other kinds of nights that are not so gentle. Everything comes out of the night, and you are the eyewitness.

You are a witness to the predation of sickness. Fevers rise and crest at night. Coughs thicken and choke. Viruses take root and rampage. Night is your vigil, to wait and hold and comfort with nothing, usually nothing, except your steadfast presence and silent faith that daylight comes and all things pass.

You will make it; you will make it to that one healthy day soon when the only thing you are nursing is a nightmare. Everything comes out of the night, and you are the eyewitness. You are a witness to fears when they take shape and find a name in your child's shadowy world. When only mom can subdue monsters and scare away spirits, when you and only you can restore peace and sweetness to the dreams beneath your child's lowered lids.

There is so much to see in the faint light of these nights. There is so much to learn about you, your child, and being human. There is the length of each night's darkness, unstirred by time or motion, filled by unseen force, traversed by the miraculous and unknowable connection between you and your child. Night after night you will wake to its pulse. You shiver, and she stirs. You worry, and she cries. You watch, and she is carried and cushioned by the invisible weight of your watching. You will be amazed at your capacity; you will be astounded by your power to respond and do anything, and your power to be still and do nothing. Everything comes out of the night, the infinity of days and nights, the vastness of things known and unknown, and you are now invited to witness it all.

The invitation comes at first several times a night. Then nightly. Then by twos and threes and then every time you need it most. The invitation is to enter eternity, with your child, with everything, into the silence of intimate stillness. To sit and to rock, to be patient and present, to be quick and compassionate, to soothe the ruffles and cool the brow, to see without seeking, to witness without ever knowing how or understanding why light follows darkness and darkness follows light.

9

Making Change

THINGS CHANGE.
HOW QUICKLY CAN YOU?

A monk asked Ummon, "What will it be when trees wither
and leaves fall?"

Ummon said, "You embody the golden breeze."

—*Blue Cliff Record*, case 27

*T*here is an illusion that this startling way of life will go
on, a new and lasting world order, so complete is the
upheaval. But things change. Just about the time you find your
footing, fooling yourself with your hard-won aplomb, circumstances change again. Your child changes minute by minute. No,
even faster: second by second. She is airborne and unburdened,
hurtling through time and space. She is the future revealing. So
are you, for that matter, but do you realize it?

The early stretch is full of false-bottomed plateaus, cruising
altitudes that lull you with their predictable rhythm of sleeping,
eating, and changing diapers. I can do this, you think. *I can do this*

forever. So profound is the illusion of permanence, so deep is our resistance to change, that we hold on to anything, even the things we can't bear. The good news is things change. Babies grow out of everything. The bad news is things change. Can *you?* How quickly can you accept change? How gracefully, how even-temperedly can you pivot and twirl, move forward or step backward? Or are you paralyzed by obstinacy?

A few months into motherhood and you're hip deep in the eternal human struggle, made worse by your own clever timing. Many of us consciously schedule motherhood for a time when we think we are done changing. We have arrived. We are stable. We've figured it all out. No more uncertainties or ambiguities for us. These are the years when we are likely to affix to a career, a partner, a home, and a hairstyle. With enough willpower and self-discipline, we can seem to forestall change for years on end—maintaining our chosen looks and pastimes, our precious privacy, our patterns and preferences, our way. We adopt beliefs, ideals, and convictions. *I know who I am,* we tell ourselves. *I know what I need.* This is the ego talking, the ego walking in a phony swagger to scare off the inevitable threats to its supremacy. Look out. Things change.

The mother of a teenager once said to me, "I remember when they're about eight months old and their ego begins to develop. It's not pretty." Neither is your own ego, and you don't have to wait eight months for it to appear! I can see now how much of motherhood, from the very first hour, carries the early warning signs of ego warfare. *I want to sleep. She wants to eat. I need to do this. She needs to do that. Not again. Again.* It can feel as though someone were eating you alive. And what is being eaten is your ego.

It seems ridiculous to talk about infant care as combat. Your baby's needs are pure and uncontrived. They are not manipulations. They are not strategic assaults. They are just assaults, relentless and evolving, against the way you want things to be. You love your child, yes, and yet you flail and roar, you cry and whine and tremble with the terror of life beyond your control.

As babies grow into toddlers, the conflicts with mom erupt and spread. Children have arms and legs and, later, words to fling at you, which they will: getting dressed, getting undressed, eating a meal, going to bed, getting in the car, getting out of the car, taking a bath, brushing teeth, and so on all day long until you both retreat, defeated, back into the night. The trick is to see the battles coming, avert them whenever possible, do what is necessary, and make peace. You can do it, you know, you're the mother, and you have infinite capacities.

I'm not talking about the parental need to impose rule and routine or to keep things safe—that's your job. I'm talking about the shocking realization that can come to you, many times a day, that you are duking it out with a ten- or twenty-pounder for no other reason than to have it your way. And your way means not budging an inch. This is deep stuff, but you don't have to dig to find it. It's right there in the craggy surface of the pits and falls of your mundane life.

The day breaks and I create an agenda. It may not appear to be self-serving, but nearly all of it is. Between the items that certainly *need* to be done are so many that I simply *want* to do because I think doing them will make me feel better, more worthy or productive. Accomplishing them gives me a sense of control against the chaos. These are false feelings, and fleeting. If I were more highly evolved I would know that everything is perfect as it is whether or not I empty the dishwasher. There is nothing wrong with wanting to empty the dishwasher. But how far will I carry this flag into the fury of the fight?

Some days, very far.

When my daughter was nearly two, for a brief and troubling time she was a head banger. Our battles would reach a pitch, sometimes instantly, and she would throw her forehead to the floor. I did the same thing at that age. *She is my daughter.* My mother told me about the first time it happened. "I was washing the dishes and you wanted to be picked up. What could I do? I needed to finish the dishes." *And I am hers.*

In a certain sense, we are all still head bangers. If your ego is unchecked (it is), you will contrive a self-serving outcome from any set of conditions (you do). Your methods of achieving this are perhaps more subtle than those of your child. Your means may seem invisible, especially to you. But for the purposes of self-awareness, what is a more repulsive and revealing representation of the ego force within each of us than a two-year-old hammering her head against the unforgiving hardwoods? No, it is not pretty.

Your child may not be the sort with a rock-hard head. You may not be either. But just for the record, there are many things you can do besides finish the dishes. Here are two: first, take a breath; second, tell yourself, *I can change.*

You can change in an instant. You can change your mind. You can change your timing. You can change your approach. You can change your words. You can laugh instead of scream. You can hop on one foot. You can step away from the fray instead of stepping in. You can give up, give in, and go in a completely different direction than you'd like to. You can do the dishes later. *What then? What next?* The Zen master has told you, "You embody the golden breeze." You *are* change. You have infinite power to relax, to release, to change, and thus to change everything. If you find that you don't have the energy or the good humor to do so this time, I will understand. There will be many opportunities afforded you.

Your child is a tireless teacher, constantly probing your self-imposed limits and boundaries, your self-centeredness, your sheer stubbornness. It is a thankless job, and who would want it? But each day your child comes to work again, taking up the monumental task.

You must be a teacher too. Of agile exits and negotiations, of quick turns and pirouettes. Of all the inventive ways to go through life instead of banging it head-on. There is a deft elegance to the mother who has mastered this dance, the dance with no choreography. She is fluid and round. She smiles and laughs easily. She breezes along as though anything were possible. Like a child.

10

Too Tired

NO RETURNS OR EXCHANGES:
FATIGUE IS THE GIFT OF THE MATERNAL

A monk asked Kyorin, "What is the meaning of Bodhidharma's coming from the West?" Kyorin said, "Sitting long
and getting tired."

—*Blue Cliff Record,* case 17

*A*void it as long as possible, then when you're ready, stop
and look at yourself in the mirror. Staring back at you
is your new best friend, your steady companion. Say hello to *fatigue.* It has come to stay.

Like all the living things in your house, it changes from day
to day and season to season. After its first few months of full do-
minion, ruling and wrecking your physical and mental health, it
retreats a bit. In its wake, you may not recognize yourself. You
have learned many important things. You have learned that sleep
is optional. You have learned that time is an illusion and that
nothing separates day from night or one day from the next. You
have learned to give up and give in. You have learned that you

can function far longer and subsist on far less than you ever imagined you would have to. And you have learned the key to eternal youth. Hint: it is not this.

I was not a wife or a mother when I attended my twentieth high school reunion. I wafted into the Marriott ballroom that night bright, shining, and weightless by the choices that had left me unencumbered at the age of thirty-eight. I looked fantastic, and more so by comparison with my classmates, I thought. Most of them were, naturally, raising families and toughing out difficult marriages. They wore every hard day's night on their faces, hair, and everywhere. An exuberant ex approached, sizing up my full effect. "What's your secret?" he gushed. I demurred. I was so deluded. I thought (a) there was a secret and (b) I knew it.

Whatever I thought it was, I must have forgotten it between the 1:00 A.M. and 4:00 A.M. feedings. I must have misplaced it on one of those ten thousand nights when the fever goes up, the coughing gets worse, or the crying won't quit. I must have washed it with the whites or swept it up with the mud, crud, and cracker crumbs.

More than the endless tasks and deprivations, it is something else that ultimately wears you down and out. It is the monumental responsibility of parenthood in general and motherhood in particular. It rises up and inhabits you, stealing every moment of self-reflection and rejuvenation. It functions within you as an alternate being, changing how you think, how you act, and what you live for. It renders you so tired, so very tired, that you begin to look and even sound like your own mother. *I am too tired to pick you up. I am too tired to play. I am too tired to laugh. I am sick and tired.*

A Zen teacher might exhort, "When you're tired, be tired." In other words, don't exaggerate, contemplate, bemoan, or otherwise *involve* yourself with it. Don't reject it; don't despise it.

Don't inflate it with meaning or difficulty. Be what you are: be tired.

Exhaustion is not a strategic spot from which to defend your turf. It's not the best place to start drawing lines and setting limits. It's not the prime state of mind for calculations of any sort. It's not a power position. And therein lies the extreme benevolence of it. Be tired. Be so tired that you will let the troubles and turmoil wash over you. Be so tired that you will stop measuring the length of your hardship and stop looking for an end. Let the encroachments advance. Lose ground. Give up another day and yet another night. Protect, defend, and guide your child, by all means, but in the main, give way.

You will forgo some things for a time—bouncy hair, brilliant eyes, clear skin, good cheer, the intoxication of looking your best—but you will lose nothing that is worth fighting for.

Fatigue is a gift. Like many of the gifts that come to mothers, it is not one you would choose, like a spa vacation, but one you can use, like a humidifier. It is a cure and a balm. Fatigue helps you forget. When you are tired, you let go. You drop what you no longer need and you do not pick it up again. You slow down. You grow quiet. You take comfort. You appreciate the smallest things. You stop fighting.

In a gentler world, the world we wish for, we would all be too tired to fight. This is perhaps the most precious gift of the maternal—a world without striving, a world at peace. In our day and time, it is an unclaimed gift. Enjoy it yourself in your own home when you are good and tired.

II

No Exit

OPEN YOUR MIND AND STEP FREE

Right before your eyes, it has always been there. Facing the situation, why don't you speak? If you don't know it in your daily life, where then will you look for it? Better find out.

—Yuanwu

*T*here we were, a bedraggled threesome in a coffee-fumed kitchen. I jostled baby Georgia on my lap as I sat at the table, skipping another breakfast because I was too full, too full already, with the burdens that bloated up out of bed every morning. My husband set his cup down and stood briskly to leave. I jerked awake. "Where are you going?" I demanded. "To the bathroom." He shrugged innocently, stunned at another of my sudden drifts onto the jagged edge.

I was jealous. I was jealous that he could respond, so agile and free, to his own urge. I was jealous that he could walk even one foot in any direction without dragging a chain. I was jealous that he could begin the day, eat a meal, leave a room, have a plan, and mind his own business. But mostly, I was jealous that he could go to the bathroom whenever he wanted.

It seems to me that a huge part of motherhood is spent looking for a parking space. Not a parking space for the car. For the kid. *Let me just find a place to put this,* you say to yourself, as though lugging one too many grocery sacks. Only it's not a sack, and there's no place else to put it. But still you look. You look for the clear counter space. You look for other arms, wind-up swings and rocking contraptions. You look for other rooms and altogether other houses. The search propels you to the park, playgroups, and preschool. Where is the spot, other than here, that I can stow this child?

When my daughter reached the miracle three-month mark (when everything does miraculously seem to settle), a filthy secret formed in my head. *I know why mothers go back to work.* It was callous, I confess. It was a cynical revelation sprung from the immense good fortune of having a choice. But the appeal was so sweet, the escape loomed so neat, that I romanced it.

I was at the health club one day (how imprisoned is that?) whining about all the obstacles in my path. I need to work, I half lied, since my need was primarily manufactured. But finding good help is so hard, I complained. Day care is good for kids, I hyped. But they get sick so much, I griped. Fed up, an onlooker cut me to the quick with: "You can wait a year to get rich."

Ow! So true. I was willing to pay almost any price just to get some green-backed gratification. How convenient that the greater share of this price would be paid by the child I would leave behind.

In the end, I did not go anywhere. I hired a part-time nanny. I felt good and I also felt guilty, and I legitimized both feelings by using the liberation to work, writing for others and for myself. Was I free? No, not often. Hour by hour, I was merely exchanging one higher value for another, one imprisoning ethic for the next. I had joined the generations of women zagging between the either and the or. *Being with my child is so important. Working is so important. Taking care of my family is so meaningful. My work is so meaningful. I should be here. I should be over there. I need to do this. I must do that. This is the right choice. No, that is the right choice.* On and on, picking, choosing, evaluating, rationalizing, and often regretting.

Remember the time you joined the health club, flush with an extra layer of resolve and motivation? I'll be in here three times a week, you assured yourself. Your discipline ebbs and flows until it flows all the way out to the Adriatic Sea. Much later you face the facts, pick up the phone, call the front office, and tell them to please stop charging your card for monthly dues; you haven't been there for more than a year.

Then there's the book group that lets you in. You're invigorated and titillated by the mere invitation to read, meet, and talk. Read, meet, and talk. After a time, you fall slack in your reading, and the talk becomes tiresome. You skip meetings. Lose my address, you wish, and the group discharges you.

There are many, many things in life that you start and then stop. Nearly everything, in fact, but this. Motherhood is a club that you cannot quit, a job you cannot shove, a prize that is nontransferable. *I know that,* you think. But then you come to *know* it, the inexhaustible dailiness, the every-nightliness. You're looking into the shadowy edges of the limitless span called "forever." You're in it, and you can't get out.

You might call a place you can't leave a prison. Is it? It is if you let it imprison you. If you dwell on what isn't. If you yearn for the halcyon past or an imagined future. Otherwise, this view right here—the droopy-eyed view from the cluttered kitchen table— is enlightenment, a glimpse at reality. This is your leaping-off point for living life as it is. Not yet ready to vault over the whys, the what-ifs, the how comes, the better offs, the remember whens? Take comfort: it is the farthest leap that a human being can make.

Today's assignment is to drop the woebegone wishes and daydreams, the ruinous comparisons to the paradise lost or aspirations unfulfilled. Tomorrow, drop them again. When you need a change, make one. When you need a break, take one. When you need help, get it. When it's time to work, work. When you need to go to the bathroom, lay your baby gently on the floor beside you, give a coo and a smile, and let 'er rip. Ah! Free at last.

PART THREE

Little by Little

CLIMB THE CLIFF
WITHOUT HANDS

12

About Time

YOU'RE THE KEEPER

Ummon said, "The world is vast and wide. Why do you put
on your seven-piece robe at the sound of a bell?"

—*Gateless Gate*, case 16

*H*ere's a word to get all worked up about: *schedule.*
Some people say babies should be on schedules.
Some say not. Everyone agrees that a schedule would be nice for
the adults lying about on call, but that's where the agreement
ends. This question of a baby schedule is not a piddling thing.
Oh, no, you'll soon find out if you haven't already: it requires al-
legiance to a chosen parenting method. Or better yet, a system.
As part of a philosophy. Inspiring a crusade. With books, semi-
nars, and support groups. Dividing moms into warring sides,
each armed to defend her irrefutable rightness and attack the ir-
redeemable wrongness of the other.

Like all wars, the battle between opposing parenting phi-
losophies is fought to win the peace—that tiny parcel of peace

between you and your baby. Put all of this ruckus in perspective and you might decide to leave the army of experts out of it and negotiate this peace yourself. If you do, you will come by a schedule the same way you arrive at anything: step by step, over and over, little by little, and on your own.

Wait a minute, you insist. You have a book that tells you otherwise. You have a book that tells you in advance the right way to bond, breast-feed, hold, respond to, and sleep with your baby in the same bed every day and night. You have a book that goes far beyond a schedule; it promises that your child will have a more successful, secure, and intelligent life if only you do what the book says.

Sounds compelling, but try to stay on neutral ground. It helps, sometimes, to be a delinquent in this debate, to leave the pages unturned, the advice unheard. It helps to be clueless.

I was clueless, and I am still grateful. Being a free agent in the parenting wars doesn't prevent difficulties or desperation, but it also doesn't delude you with dogma. It doesn't lure you into thinking you know something when you don't. It doesn't multiply your doubts when reality diverges from your expectations. It doesn't hold you back from trying things a different way. Above all, it doesn't blind you to the obvious. More than analyzing theories or applying techniques, arriving at a schedule is about recognizing the obvious.

Of course, it takes time to see things as they really are.

During her hospital stay, the nurses fed Georgia on a three-hour schedule. As she ate more at a feeding (a whopping two ounces!), she graduated to every four hours. She had hit a milestone in the neonatal curriculum, and *voilá,* she was discharged smack dab into my dunderheaded care.

"I think I'll just keep her on that four-hour schedule," I

mused as we drove to the hospital to bring her home. I was already imagining her rapid progress up the curve. *Four hours, five hours, fork and spoon.* The doctor there nearly laughed when I asked the question just to confirm my good sense. "Oh, no, at home you'll feed her on demand," she corrected.

Demand? She was a four-pound three-ounce cricket, still four weeks shy of full-term consciousness, and I hadn't as yet detected a single demand. That changed as she approached what had been her original due date. Her growing awareness of her growing belly, when it was growing empty, put the world in motion. So this is what a newborn does! Empty tummies are a time bomb. Babies schedule themselves, and you simply don't get a say, not at first.

Wait a minute, you insist again. You have a book that tells you otherwise. You have a book that tells you just what you want to hear when you see for yourself what an awful lot of bother real babies are. You have a book that speaks volumes to the sleep deprived. It says things like: *Parents matter, too! You are the boss! Train your baby now!* And more than a book, you have a friend who has a friend who testifies that the method really works and after the crying stops, her baby goes to sleep smiling.

Sounds appealing, but try to stay on neutral ground.

Soon your baby will enter a stage when he is more than just a hunger pang. He is awake. He moves about. He can be engaged and entertained. And you ask yourself, "Are we on a schedule?" You ask your fellow mothers, "Are you on a schedule?" You all confess, "We're not on a schedule yet." Yippee! No one is scoring in the bonus rounds yet.

I read in one of those books of yours (I peeked) that if I kept track of the time and amount of my baby's meals and the time and duration of her naps, a schedule would appear. I have two spiral notebooks, with all the times and measurements, for 365 days, and while she never missed a meal, nothing *appeared* on those hen-scratched pages. But something does appear over time, and when it does, it appears right in front of your eyes.

Did you ever notice that summer follows spring? That April follows March? Wednesday follows Tuesday? That sunset follows sunrise? And that it does so every day with such extreme predictability that the exact times can be calculated with flawless precision and printed in an almanac a year in advance? All of life is balanced on the precise and predictable unfolding of events. Your child's life is no exception.

Are you aware that your breathing weaves a uniform pattern, your heart beats in faultless cadence, and your body functions in continuous, self-regulated flow? Your baby doesn't need you to impose a schedule, least of all one from a Web site or a book; your baby *is* a schedule of sequential events at predictable times. What she needs is for you to *see* it. Your baby doesn't need an imperious schedule maker but an attentive timekeeper.

This is your new spiritual practice: telling time. Fortunately for both of you, this practice brings many rewards.

Zen students regularly participate in extended meditation retreats, which are called sesshins. The aim of a sesshin is to put aside your self-centered preoccupations and clear your mind so you can see things as they are. A sesshin might last three, seven, ten, or many more days, but during sesshin each day is the same. Sesshin days follow a schedule originated in Japanese Zen monasteries and based on thousands of years of observing human functioning. The schedule combines periods of sitting meditation with walking meditation, chanting, chores, rest, and meals. All activities follow in the same orderly sequence and occur each day at the same hour. Time is marked by the timekeeper, who ceremonially rings a bell at the beginning and the end of allotted periods. Every time a bell rings, you know exactly what to do. With a few days of practice, you know exactly what to do when there are no bells. Your mind is clearing, and you are more aware.

This sounds quaint. What is not quaint is the murderous rage you feel, at first, as your ego flares up against the discipline. We don't like to be ruled by the clock, or anything else for that matter. We like to be in charge of our own time: to own it, use it, waste it, lose track of it, and sleep through it. We like to sneak in, out, and around time. We like to be early; we like to be late; we like what we like when we like it! *The world is vast and wide,* our reasoning goes, *why be entrapped by a timepiece?*

A few days into the iron-walled refuge of a sesshin, your resistance starts to dissipate and you notice something remarkable. You thought you'd feel lousy, but you feel better. You used to stay up all hours, but now you're nodding off at 9:00 P.M. You never used to rest, but you've been napping. At first you were exhausted, but now you feel energized. You're usually late, but you've been on time. You habitually skip meals, but three squares a day never tasted so good. At this point, more bells go off. So this is what it feels like to live a healthy life!

Isn't this all you really want for your child? When you begin to take notice, it becomes clear what to do about time.

You'll notice the time when you can drop the early-morning feeding and replace it with a solid-food "breakfast." You'll notice the time when you can delay the late-afternoon snack and combine it into "dinner." You'll notice the times when your child is tired. If you tell yourself that your child never acts tired, you will have many more times to see how your child acts when he is tired.

When my daughter passed infancy and started freestyling toward toddlerhood, her voluntary napping disappeared, or diminished into odd times and inconvenient places. My instincts told me that sleeping was inherently good for her; her deteriorating temperament told me when she had passed her breaking point. Would she easily give in to repose? Not on your life. There is a benevolent power in parenthood, and I believe napping is one place it should be exercised.

Developmental guidelines say a ten-month-old should be napping twice a day, morning and afternoon. My spiral notebook told me that she was dozing here and there and sometimes never. Why? Perhaps because I had never created a nap time. Most babies don't do that themselves; mommies do. So one day I watched for signs that she was tired, even in the midst of her nonstop activity—a wipe of her eye, a sudden tear burst. Bells went off. One at midmorning. One at midafternoon. It was nap time. I ritualized it with a routine: milk, stories, rocking, and whispered songs in a darkened room. Asleep she fell, my sweet girl. Every day at the same hour. Every time in the same way. She became predictable when I became predictable.

We had finally arrived at a schedule, one that would naturally grow and change as she did. At every step it was up to *me* to notice it in *her*, mark the time, and put myself on a schedule. When you do this, I promise you that every day, as the clock ticks, you'll both know exactly what time it is.

Not long ago I met a gray and gracious woman at the park, where her four-year-old granddaughter rambled with Georgia. She remembered her own first days with her babies as though it were Wednesday last.

> I had the two boys. Twins. I used to ask, "Oh, my Lord, why me?" If I could get the wash going by nine in the morning, why then . . . I'd clean the dirty diapers into the toilet and soak them in the tub. We had the tub by the

washer back then, and these were cloth diapers. If I could get the wash going by nine, and then hung on the line, then I could get organized. I had to get organized by nine. And I learned that I was good at organizing.

She recalled this clockwork as though it were her finest hour. "I'm past seventy-two," she said later, leaving me to guess whether she meant months or years past. The strength and certainty were still with her. Her secret to doing it was doing it on time.

Is this such a rare and insightful teaching? I don't know, but on those nights when my husband and I are out catching a late dinner or a movie, we often find ourselves bobbing through a sea of strollers carting strung-out toddlers into the middle of the night. *My child never sleeps. My child never eats.* These refrains are like a new national anthem. It makes me wonder. Where did we lose the rhythm and flow from morning to noon to night? The iridescent beat of sunrise, the soothing tempo of twilight? The irrefutable day and inviolate night? Who took away time? It's up to you to find it.

I am devoted to the schedule. I am devoted to routine to maintain physical and mental health. For my daughter, yes, but above all for me. The structure lends security. The focus gives me sanity. The predictability begets, in a paradoxical way, freedom. The simple ceremony of ritualized activity dignifies our ordinary lives. We eat our cereal and then we wash our bowls. We brush our teeth and then we comb our hair. We put on our socks and then our shoes. Perfect mastery, moment after moment.

As my daughter has grown older, I have seen how useful my compulsion has been to her. It reassures her that, even when it's not entirely on her terms, her life is predictable and safe. And as

I have grown wiser, I have likewise seen when my compulsion serves no one, when it provokes needless urgency and anxiety rather than calm. That's when it's time to unwind myself from the clock and appreciate life's unpredictability.

On a perfect day in your perfect little world (and it's always perfect) there is breakfast time, playtime, lunchtime, nap time, snack time, dinnertime, bath time, story time, and bedtime. There is time for everything when you are the timekeeper.

13

Other Toys

KNOW HOW TO BE SATISFIED

Desires are inexhaustible
I vow to put an end to them.

—The Bodhisattva Vows

*O*ne day in a Lutheran church in Texas, a miracle
happened.

I had taken Georgia on a trip to see my mother, who was
undergoing chemotherapy for her ovarian cancer. We had carefully timed our visit for one of the rare "good" weeks, which
were only good in comparison to the other weeks of fever, nau-
sea, and total incapacitation. At seven months old, my daughter
would be baptized. The faith was not my own; it was not my husband's. All things considered, that mattered not one whit. The
baptism was a gift. But it was not the miracle.

During the middle of the service, I took my restless girl into
the church nursery. There, bobbing in the middle of the room,

was a contraption known to cognoscenti as a baby saucer. This was not the kind of thing that would ever land on my wish list. I thought they were hideous and huge, and I could not imagine giving up half of my living room to yet another baby thing, especially one combining all the crude amusements of a video arcade: garish colors, spinning balls, whizzers, and bells. Then the miracle happened: Georgia liked it. I thought to myself: *Hallelujah! I want to make her happy.*

Home again, I went straight to Sears and charged the sixty-dollar model. I impressed upon my husband the urgency of assembling it that night. He did; we rearranged the furniture.

She never willingly sat in it again. Oh, I'm sure there was a time or two. In a pinch, I would plop her there for the half second before her screaming began. I thought: *Maybe I should get the ninety-nine-dollar one.*

This was my first experience with the rule called Other People's Toys. The emphasis is on the "other." You like them precisely because they are not yours. The corollary to this rule is Other People's Kids, precocious and polite, who make you think: *Why can't my kid be more like that?*

We held on to the baby saucer for a while and then priced it to sell at a garage sale. I hope it delivered hours and hours of saucer happiness and satisfaction to generations of families thereafter. For me it was the beginning of an up-close analysis of human desire as expressed by Georgia. What I saw was that her desires were spontaneous, impermanent, and never ending. When she wanted something now it only meant that she wanted something now. Desires change. Satisfaction eludes. That's what it means to be human, with infinite, insatiable desires. It's not about the saucer! It did start me thinking: *I want to have a separate playroom.*

I tried to keep the big picture in mind when we went to

Other People's Houses and played with Other People's Kids and Other People's Toys. I'd see Georgia clutch something, somebody else's something, with the fervor of new-car fever. I didn't have to buy it. She didn't have to own it. It would probably never come up again. Still, I thought: *I wish she could learn to share.*

This lesson took full form when she was slightly older and we'd leaped over that high-minded wall to watching children's TV. The commercial kind. I would shudder as the hard sell washed over us in waves, gasping as my daughter pointed to every plastic, pink, and shiny thing, "I want that. I want that. I want that. I want that." She was, in her plaintive and *almost* irresistible way, giving voice to innumerable human desires. It wasn't about the Barbie Color Curls Styling Head! (*Thank God,* I thought. *I want her to have classic old-fashioned wooden educational toys handmade from centuries-old patterns by artisans in remote Oregon workshops.*)

In time the TV would go off. And so would she. On to newer news and other others. Her cravings could be extinguished by remote control. Not so, mine.

At this age, your child doesn't have the kind of ruminating, obsessive mind that you have. Your child's desires do not involve implicit judgments of what is good and what is bad. They are not based on biased evaluations of what he has and what he doesn't, what he likes and what he hates. Your child's desires are not yet masked by self-deceit and benign code words. Sure, the occasional tantrum and whining are hard to bear, but an unsatisfied child does not yet create the monstrous havoc of an unsatisfied parent. Parents of preschoolers say that one of their biggest problems is how to manage the tasteless, media-planted desires spewing from the mouths of their babes. It might be worthwhile, while the remote control is still firmly in your grasp, to shift some of your concern to the more subtle and insidious desires of your own—the desires that are far harder to turn off because you don't even acknowledge that you have them.

Inexhaustible desires are the silent subtext to our whole lives, including life as a parent. *I want, I want, I want.* We spend nearly every minute wanting things to be a little bit different, a little bit better. Even now, reading this, you might be thinking defensively: *But I only want what's best.*

We call it wanting the "best." We say we want "advantages" for our children. We say we are "enriching" their environment and "exposing" them to more "opportunities." That's all well and good, but what do we mean when we say that? Do we mean that we want them to turn out smarter? More talented? More popular? More attractive? More admired? More successful? More accomplished? With more status and money? Yes! We mean all of that and more! To what end? To serve whom? To serve ourselves? So we can be satisfied? We won't be satisfied then unless we know how to be satisfied now.

What do we mean by all these things we want "for our children"? All these things we think they "need"? Whatever they are, and however we acquire these things, the fact remains: desires are inexhaustible. Chasing them, however, will exhaust *you.* It will frustrate you. It will cause worry and anxiety, grumbling and dissatisfaction. It will disrupt your home and impose expectations on those around you. It will cost you money, and it will cost you time, all the while distracting you from your life, bountiful and precious, right in front of you. As it does that, it will cause sickness. Just listen to yourself wailing, "I want, I want, I want" (or just listen to me), and see if it doesn't make you feel sick.

All of us have seen these kinds of mothers: anxious for their kids to catch on, catch up, move on, move up, be first in line, be next in line, be ahead of the curve, be better, have it all. All of us have seen these kinds of kids: bombarded with the best, assaulted with all the advantages, herded from one opportunity to the next, overdosed on exposure, starving on enrichment, and haunted by the endless dissatisfactions of their parents.

I have seen these kinds of mothers; I have seen that I am one.

And sometimes, only rarely, I see beyond my ravenous appetites to realize that all of my needs are already met. I have the opportunity to gently remind myself that desires are inexhaustible and vow once again to put an end to them. To fulfill that vow, I have the advantage of hearing Buddha's teaching: *Want little, and know how to be satisfied.* And I should know how to be satisfied, because I have already been given the most precise and effective means to enrich my life: by not adding one thing to it! Not one more wish, not one more want, not one more thought. I can let desires, as they will, come up; and I can let them, as they will, go away, providing I don't chase them all the way to Sears for the higher-priced model. I can trust that everything my family truly needs—every opportunity my daughter needs to fulfill herself—is already present and will be. Satisfaction is never the future outcome of some hoped-for event. Satisfaction always lies right where you are.

When I cannot evoke the even-mindedness to *really* know this, I can try to live *as if* I do. To that same end, I invite you to do some difficult things with your child. Turn the TV off. Throw the catalogs away. Even for the sake of literacy, don't try to entertain your toddler by giving her toy catalogs and calling them magazines, as I once did. Take and use hand-me-downs; give even more yourself. Detour around the mall; it is not a free or safe playground no matter how bored the both of you are. Have garage sales, and size up the true value of your valuables. When your closets are full and your baby is too little to expect otherwise, write at the bottom of the birthday-party invitation, "no gifts."

There is nothing wrong with a gift or a toy, but don't append any extra value to any of them as needed or educational. It is the things we don't have, after all, that are truly educational. They help us to see the chains of our dissatisfaction and, ultimately, encourage us to step free. What a priceless gift to the ones we love.

14

Flowers Fall

WHEN BAD THINGS HAPPEN

> Yet in attachment blossoms fall, and in aversion weeds spread.
>
> —Dogen Zenji, "Actualizing the Fundamental Point"

*I*f you are a good mother, a *really good* mother, nothing bad will ever happen to your child.

You will hold that floppy little neck just so and never let it loll. You will prop her to sleep only in the safe way and never let her roll. You will be a fierce guardian at the gate, keeping slobbery kids and dogs at a distance. When it is time, you will eradicate every risk and danger in the house, rig the drawers and cabinets, remove the pharmaceuticals and solvents, replace the untempered glass, fence off the stairs, bolt the toilet, bar the VCR, cushion everything hard and mean, because the world, it now seems, is such a menacing place, such a vicious and menacing place. But you've done your best; you have the proof in every latch and lock that you *are* a really good mother.

When that illusion cracks, when it slips and scuffs, when it falls and rips open, when you hold the broken tooth or the scalded finger, when an ice cube and a kiss don't stop the blood, when you drive fast and hard into the night to the fluorescence of the nearest emergency room, when you hold and rock the pain and screams, that's when you will know what mothering requires of you.

Oh, if it were only a matter of forethought, prevention, and a little hardware.

Most of us live endowed by good fortune and status: as though we will live forever. We live fiercely fortified by the illusion of inalienable rights, among them the right to perfection. So ingrained are these expectations that when something goes kablooie we judge it to be either (a) a faulty model or (b) a faulty operator, but definitely a fault. And for every fault there must be detection, prevention, and remedy, or wherefore the modern science of total quality management?

This is the absolutism, the certitude, with which we divide our view of the world. The either and or, the good and bad, the better and worse, the right and wrong, the sickness and health, the perfect and imperfect, the before and after, the flower and weed, the you and me. In Buddhism this is called dualism, the view of everything as part of a pair of opposites. The world, of course, does not really divide that way, only our egocentric views do. By *good,* we mean good for *me.* By *wrong,* we mean wrong to *me.* Ask your child to distinguish between a daisy and a dandelion to see that there is no distinction at all. We call it a weed because we don't like it; we call it a flower because we do; we call it a tragedy because flowers fall. And so it is in life. So it is!

Georgia was nearly two when I called to her one evening from another room. "Bath time!" I sang out, knowing that it would unleash her body and soul into my command. At that age, she had such exuberance for the new, anything new, that just announcing the start of something new would send her rocketing forth. It was my way to get her to do what I wanted.

She came running down the hall toward the carpeted room where, smug with the success of this happy transition, I waited. She barreled in, stubbed her toe on the high pile underfoot, and fell forward against a metal bed frame. There was a pause before I heard the cry, unlike any other I'd yet heard, deep and full, powered by something other than oxygen. I grabbed her and held her close because I was too afraid to look at her precious, perfect face.

But I did. I did look at her face, and afterward, I did everything else I needed to do for my lovely, bleeding girl, to stay with and stand beside her, to reassure and strengthen her, to share the terrible fear and hurt of the awful ordeal that unfolds when accidents happen. We were so lucky to have, as a friend and neighbor, a doctor, a father himself, of Georgia's playmate Emily. He answered the phone and came down the street in seconds, looked at the cut on her forehead that would not close, told us quickly *I hate to tell you this,* put us all in his confident hands, and drove us to his office to sew her up.

She was, for me, the first child ever to have endured what she did—the straitjacketed terror of having your head stitched up while your mommy pins you down in place. She was, in truth, one of the last, because soon after this, surgical glue would replace stitches for skin-deep cuts like hers.

We recovered. Of course we all recovered. She would point to her scar and tell the story with its happy baby-talk ending, "Emmy's daddy fix it." We got rid of the culprit metal-framed bed. Life went on, and we tucked the episode between the "before" and the "after."

My mother's first round of chemotherapy was successful, or so it seemed to us. She revived. Her hair sprouted. Her vigor returned and she went searching for something, anything, that could restore what she could no longer conjure up: feeling like she did before. Before chemo? Before surgery? Before the *c* word? Before carcinogens, cyclamates, hormone replacement therapy, or second-hand smoke? Before the first cell made its disastrous detour toward mutation? She tried acupuncture, herbs, juices, vitamins, music, laughter, meditation, and some of the old wives' tales and remedies sent her way. I didn't tell her there was no "before," no place, no time, no single fixed point of certain health, certain safety, or certain anything. I didn't tell her because I, too, wanted her to find it. Hope springs even as flowers fall.

When I went to Los Angeles to meditate with Maezumi Roshi for the first time, it was, by coincidence, the weekend of my thirty-seventh birthday. I told him the occasion, but otherwise I was covering up a lot that weekend, or so I thought—my heartache, my loneliness, my endless longing, and my fear of moving beyond. He gave me a handmade gift: a freshly inked calligraphy of the kanji Chinese characters for *spring* and *fall*.

"Would you like to see my inspiration?" he offered, and he pointed to a line of delicate print in a leather-bound volume, where I read: *No matter how much the spring wind loves the peach blossoms, they still fall.*

"Do you understand it?" He smiled.

"No"; I hid again. I understood it to the bone, just as he had understood me.

"Then let that be your koan," he replied. Let that be your teaching; let that be your life. So it is, and it is sometimes sad.

There would be many more falls and hurts, health scares and

78

panics. There would be dire test results and ominous CAT scans. There is so very much to learn about this life by its fragility. I could make my daughter safer, but I could not keep her safe. Nor could I do anything for my mother but love her, knowing fuller each day the things that love cannot overcome. Like gravity.

I let Georgia lie in my arms and wet my shoulder with her sobs. Wherever the pain and sorrow take her, I will go too. That's what a momma's for. That's what it's all about.

15

Workloads

WHO'S THE REAL WORKHORSE
IN THE FAMILY?

If you find one thing wearisome, you will find everything
wearisome.

—Dogen Zenji, "Guidelines for Studying the Way"

*I*n the midst of my drudgery, I look up and wonder where
the good times went.

When I walked away from my career to create a family,
my colleagues kidded that I was "retiring to a life of cats and
flowers." So true, so true. And cat hair and pollen dust, fleas and
weevils, stains and stink, sanitizing and deodorizing, boiling,
wiping, scraping, scrubbing, loading, folding, mending, mound-
ing, hounding, and work, work, work.

Funny, I felt the same way every day at the office.

We can walk away from our jobs yet leave hardly a thing behind, because we bring our discriminating mind with us—the
mind that values and devalues, weighs and critiques, complains

and compares. Now, as then, nearly every day I feel overwhelmed
and out of time. Often I feel the work is beneath me. Often I feel
the work is beyond me. It must be important to me to feel that
way. It must be important to me to think of my life as hard work
and myself as a workhorse. Sometimes it feels good to feel so
bad; it feels high to feel so low.

Early in my Zen practice, I attended a retreat and was given
the job of ringing a handheld bell as the priest entered the meditation hall to perform services, three times a day. The entry and
exit ritual required that I ring this little bell fourteen times,
blending with the rhythm of other bells and bows in the ceremony—a tricky bit of orchestration. As you might expect from
what I've told you, this job was very hard work for me, and I
worked hard at it. I didn't just work at it the *fourteen seconds* during each service that my little bell was to sound; I worked at it all
day and night. I worked at it in my head, in my sleep, and under
my breath, working and reworking to arrive at the ideal beat,
working and reworking in pursuit of the right ring. It was ex-
hausting, but I never quit working at it.

Toward the end of the retreat, the teacher asked me if I was
ready to advance my practice by moving into the study of koans,
the ancient teaching stories used in my Zen tradition to deepen
meditation. "I can't possibly do that," I answered sincerely, my
mind ringing with *ching*s. "I'm already doing the bell."

He nodded in complete understanding.

"You seem to have a little problem with your work ethic,"
he said. I didn't follow, since I judged myself to be the hardest
worker there ever was.

"You make *everything* work," he said.

I do. Do you?

When you are scraping the crusted cereal from the wall
with a chipped fingernail, do not think: *For this I gave up a vice*

presidency. When you are folding a stack of late-night laundry, do not think: *This is my sixth load this week and it's only Monday.* When you stand over a sink of three-day-old dishes, do not think: *When, oh when, will I ever catch up?* And while you're at it, please don't complain about the mindless nature of a mother's work. The great transformative potential of a mother's work is that it *is* mindless. No thinking of any kind is required.

Now you know when I got the hang of that bell.

Back in the wee months, when I faced up to the fact that Georgia would be drinking more from a bottle than from a breast, I called a girlfriend who had taken this route ahead of me and asked her how she did it. I was looking for a system, some way to streamline what loomed as an impossibly complicated and time-consuming ordeal. "Every night I boiled the bottles and the nipples, then boiled the water and mixed the powder and filled the bottles and stored them in the refrigerator for the next day," she told me. *You did? Every night? Twelve bottles?* I could hardly believe it. This was more work than anything I'd heard of in my twenty-year career of intensely hard work. Where's the technology? Where's the automation? Where's the one-touch activation? We lived in a world where you could clear your driving record in a single visit to the Web Traffic School, but moms were still boiling bottles past midnight? Where's the twenty-first century? It didn't occur to me that I was making work out of this teensy, repetitive, and even meditative motion, so important was it to me to do everything the hard way.

If you ever manage to stop *working* so hard, you might let your tired eyes alight on the real workhorse in the family. It will surprise and even delight you.

What children will accomplish from birth to age three is astounding. Try not to overlook this most amazing teaching. You'll be inclined to, because children greet each day with glee and fearlessness. Their instinctive joy does not mean that the work of a child is easy or discountable. It does mean that life, as my teacher tried to tell me, is more fun than we sometimes make it.

Your child's physical transformation alone is astounding, and their quest for physical mastery is inspiring. Imagine if you set out, in one year, to learn trapeze flying, downhill skiing, and ballet dancing. You would fall a lot. You would hurt yourself. You might cry. Would you never ever give up?

Far more daunting, I believe, are the cognitive and behavioral skills on the syllabus. Yes, it's said that "two" is terrible, but can you consider the course load for a minute? Self-feeding and table skills, language, emotional management, toilet training, and social etiquette, for starters. And all occurring amid the frightening undertow toward separation and independence. Throw in weaning, the big bed, and assorted other traumatic transitions such as a new sibling, babysitter, or preschool, whenever they enter the picture. These kids are working in the coal mine!

And still your child will wake up each day, with only rare exceptions, beaming and eager. Unburdened by the weight of things she has yet to do, your child is never overwhelmed and never underequipped. There's plenty of time for everything, even when there's no tomorrow!

Me, I cling ferociously to my hurriedness and shorthandedness. The day is potholed from divots of despair I churn up and then trip over. Do you think that *I* could learn to keep from falling down?

In a year or so, when your child begins to *play* in earnest imitation of all your hard work washing, cleaning, and cooking, perhaps the point will come home.

Meanwhile, consider all of this as a way to conjure up more

empathy on an ordinary day. Yes, we all have a load on our hands, but the *heavy* is in our heads. Set the heavy down and sweep aside the useless mental clutter. Don't think of a single reason why you can't go out for ice cream. Two scoops—who's counting?

When you can do anything as though you work at nothing, you have the best days of your life.

16

Just Eat

LET FOOD BE FOOD

> To study and practice the inheritance of the Buddha's ancestral wisdom is to bring forth the vital activity of having rice.
>
> —Dogen Zenji, "Everyday Activity"

*T*here are moments of sublime and intoxicating fulfillment in motherhood when all of your doubts give way to a deep and radiating certainty that you are succeeding.

One of these moments is when your child sleeps. Another is when your child poops. And the third—perhaps most gratifying of all—is when your child eats. This gives you an excellent idea of what passes for pleasure in our house.

The satisfaction that I experience as I finagle my baby to gargle down a spoonful of pureed peas is so elevating, so empowering, so altogether *delicious,* that it becomes obvious: there's something more on this plate than peas.

When you're not looking, you will spoon-feed your child all

of your hang-ups about food. Even if you are looking, you will still do it. Because there is not a single one of us unenlightened beings to whom food is just food. When is a pea no longer a pea? When it is love, nurturing, comfort, and bliss. When it is good, right, pure, wholesome, and certified. When it is weird, exotic, unattractive, sinful, and forbidden. When it is an accomplishment or when it is a failure. When it is a tool to control, impose, coerce, reward, or punish. And when it substitutes for entertainment, activity, company, consolation, conversation, or anything that isn't spelled p-e-a.

We think this is part of our job: to teach children how to eat. Our children invariably suffer for it. They are lucky we don't likewise believe it is our job to teach them how to breathe.

To be fair, there is the acquired knowledge of drinking from cups and using utensils, sitting at a table and eating from one's own plate. These are social skills; when they are physically able, children will learn these rather refined behaviors in the rather refined situations like the six times a year you sit down at the table and have a family meal. For all the preaching about whole wheat and organics; for all the vexations about salt, preservatives, chemicals, and juice from concentrate; for all the fixations on sugar; for all the kitchen-table conspiracies to introduce, offer, camouflage, convince, trick, and bribe; for all the wailing and gnashing about how to get our children to *just eat,* they will continue to demonstrate how they can *just eat* fine without any impositions from us. Until we contaminate their food and eradicate their appetite with all of our extra helpings of anxiety, it's quite simple. A pea is just a pea.

When our babies are babies, we wouldn't think of wedging ourselves between their searching lips and the ready nipple. They know when to eat, they know how to eat, and they just eat! This is called ancestral wisdom. They are natural-born buddhas! This is not wisdom they lose, although we can help them forget it, just as we have.

When my daughter entered the arena of "solid" foods, it had all the markings of a new playing field—one where I wore the whistle, carried the clipboard, and called the shots. There were whole chapters and books on this topic. Doctors to consult and old wives to tell. Charts and diagrams. Ingredients to read and brand names to favor. Methods and measurements. I didn't see this as just an everyday activity. I saw it as a maternal mission: engineering a *good* eater.

Yes, we get to choose the food. We get to procure and prepare it. We put it in the bowl and scoop it on the spoon, but we don't stop where we should. We push an agenda. We shovel and prod. We cajole and coddle. We coo in pleasure and furrow in frustration. We try one thing and then another. We keep it up until we've had our fill of either success or failure. The kid eats, but mainly, we're feeding our egos on pabulum and peas.

As parents we become so personally invested in our kids' eating that we will push anything, even the hard stuff, as long as it is on a spoon. *Finish your cake, Georgia! Have one more bite of ice cream!* These inanities have actually been spoken at our table, and no doubt will be many more times. I am peddling food nonstop, but it is the rare occasion when I catch and stop myself in the act.

Letting food be food means that when your child eats, that's all there is to it. When he doesn't eat, that's all there is to it. When he has a cookie, that's all there is to it. When he has homemade steamed organic yams mashed by your doting hands, that's all there is to it.

But oh, how we think there's a lot more to it! There are complications and repercussions, we think. There are vitamins and minerals, thiamin and niacin. There's perfect teeth and healthy skin and building strong bones twelve ways. There's brain food, for goodness' sake. There are additives, allergies, and sugar! There are the ramifications of enriching the corporate baby food empires or sustaining the local food co-ops. There's cow or soy, tap or bottled. Did I mention sugar? Why not vegetarianism? You have to weigh this aspect against that aspect and consider the long-range impact and the short-term consequence and so on and so on. Thinking parents have a lot on their plate.

If these sound like some of your issues, then you have a home where food is an issue. Keep piling your issues on the table and soon a child who tries to just eat won't be eating any longer. She'll be pushing back in a power struggle to escape your heavy-handed intentions. There will be power struggles anyway, but you'd all be better off if they didn't play out over pork and beans.

That doesn't mean that food isn't useful. Sometimes, in order to get from point A to point C, you have to take the drive-thru at point B and toss some french fries to the toddler in the back-seat. When Georgia resisted using the potty to deposit her no. 2s, the nurse suggested—with a scientific basis—that M&M's might cinch the deal. These are expedient means.

Nearly 750 years ago, Dogen quoted the teaching of his master, Tendo Nyojo, on enlightenment: *When hunger comes, have rice.*

Most of us are far removed from this kind of vital and undistracted activity, as easy as it sounds. We never just eat when we eat, our attention is elsewhere—we gab, read, plan, debate, discuss, drive, or maybe keep working. We may never feel hunger—chomping and chugging absentmindedly throughout the day and into our beds at night. When it comes to eating, we are out to lunch. But there's a guru in that booster seat.

When Georgia was two, we joined an afternoon playgroup where every day the children sat on teeny chairs at a teeny table and were offered a nutritious, age-appropriate snack. We parents sat on the perimeter, stifling the impulse to speak out and take charge authoritatively. *My child won't sit at a table!* All the children sat. *My child won't eat!* The children politely refused what they did not want, asked for what they did want, and ate. *My child doesn't eat that much!* They often asked for more. Invited to pour their own drinks, the kids served themselves water from a measuring cup. *My child can't manage that!* Every child did. Spills were wiped up without comment. No one prodded them to eat, to eat more, or to finish everything. They just ate. When they judged themselves finished, they were asked to carry their plates and cups to a nearby trash can before resuming play. *Now that's something my child will definitely never do!* Every one of them, every time, bused his or her own table. To the adults, snack was a resounding success. To the kids, it was just snack.

The wisdom of your child's self-feeding instinct is already perfect. When the doctors reassure, "Children do not starve themselves," it sounds like a patronizing put-down, especially when you are locked in a losing battle every day at the table. Yet it sums up the matter. Life sustains itself. It goes on and grows on, breathing and eating, sleeping, peeing and pooping. As moms, we can implicate and congratulate ourselves as much as we want, but we don't have that much to do with it. We can't ever understand it, get ahead of it, or control it, but we sure can mess it up. A friend once hollered, "If I can't control what my kid eats, what can I control?" That's one of those questions that answer themselves in the hush that follows.

Make sensible, timely, varied meals. Try new things. Try old things. Pay the slightest attention and you'll have a hunch what to offer and when. Make no assumptions and have no expectations about what your child will eat. Bite your tongue about your own likes, dislikes, cravings, aversions, and addictions. Curb your own compulsions. Don't spread the eating habits you detest in yourself. Learn, anew, how to recognize when you are hungry and do other things when you are not.

Then, just eat. If you don't know what I mean, watch your little one. Left to their own impulses, children will certainly put food in its proper place.

17

On and Off

TUNING IN TO THE MIDDLE WAY

If you wish to know the truth,
then hold to no opinions for or against anything.

—Seng-t'san, "Verses on the Faith-Mind"

*T*V or not TV? Oh, yes, the question of the day. The question of every day.

There are easy ways to answer it. One is, don't own a TV. The second is, if your TV breaks, don't replace it. The third is, give away a TV if it comes into your possession. For the rest of us, the issue is as precarious as a two-wheeler without training wheels. It's all in the balance.

Most of us lean emphatically one way at first. Absolutely not, no way, no sir, no TV before age three at the earliest! Our infants are sleeping for the greater part of this period of moral certainty. And then there comes the day when your child wakes up; the phone rings; the sink backs up; the microwave catches on fire; you are starving, thirsty, stinky, done in, dead tired; your conviction is tested, and you totter.

Any or none of these things has to happen for you to find yourself doing what I did. One day, when my husband was ensconced in the sanctuary of his morning shower, I decided to take charge of my wormlike existence. Today, I said to myself, I will bathe before 9:00 P.M. I will dress for the day. In fact, I will do it right now, by putting her right here, in the safety of her beloved bouncer chair, attended by the engaging and educational stimulation of Barney!

When I emerged, clean and steamy from my moment's bliss, my husband stood before me gaping in disbelief and condemnation. It was an indefensible sight. The bouncer chair was eerily still. Georgia, a babbler, was stone silent. Barney was warbling and she was in the zone. I rushed to her, to her dilated pupils and puddling drool. I saw it then: this is a bad thing. This is a very bad thing.

What did we do? Nothing. We didn't give away our TV. When it broke, we replaced it. Still, we'd seen into the mouth of the hulking purple monster, and we kept a safer distance. The videos given for her first birthday inspired our terror. Harmless kiddie songs and furry puppets— that's what *you* think! We kept them under lock and key. *Thank you so much for your gift of baby's first small-caliber weapons.*

Time and circumstance work on these situations like a river on a rock. The hard edges wear away. You soften up. It's a good thing, too. Our daughter wasn't living in an ideologically pristine world. The door was not barred. The air was unpurified. This wasn't a case study and we weren't lab rats. She was living in our world, in our house, with a thirty-six-inch Sony in the living room. By making this choice, or rather, by making no choice, we put ourselves on a more difficult path than prohibition. We had chosen Zen's middle way, the path free of discriminating views. (Translation: We still watch *Survivor.*)

We are exercising moderation, and that takes a lot of exercise. It requires much more effort and diligence, much more involvement and attention than either extreme. It's so easy to be lazy about how much TV your child sees, but that creates addiction. It's also easy to be rigidly prohibitive, but that creates craving. It's much easier to hold an opinion either way than to hold a remote control, take responsibility for pushing "on" and "off," and fess up to the consequences.

Opinions are funny things. Most parents agree that TV is a dulling, exploitative, and mildly wicked influence on our children. Most parents agree that a plasma screen provides superb picture quality and crisp sound with low distortion from almost any angle. See? Opinions can conflict, provoke, confuse, and contradict each other—and these are just the opinions that you hold yourself. Opinions are fine for the purpose of discussion or the sport of debate, but they don't work in the real world. *You* are what works in the real world.

Depending on the time and the conditions, TV can be a lifesaver or a life taker. Many a time TV has saved my child when her intemperate mom was ready to bite or bolt or both. Many a time I have let ten minutes of the tube ooze on languorously until my daughter's entire being evaporated into vacuity. You must be present to discern when one situation transforms into the other. You must be present if you wish to know the truth. You simply must be present.

All of the same can be said for the multitude of media diversions that now infiltrate our lives and occupy every corner of our homes. Be watchful that you do not install a TV in your child's room. Be watchful that you do not take pride in her precocious ability to load a VCR or activate the DVD player. Be watchful that you do not grant an exemption from all of this watchfulness to time your child spends at the computer, which you will. The latest technology always seems to trump commonsense precautions and invite ridiculous double standards. Even without the home theater system our husbands want for Christmas, our houses are already temples of electronic stimulation. We as parents must be the temple guards.

Be forewarned: there's nothing moderate about moderation. It takes a lot of practice. Moderation demands that you never ever fool yourself, but you will keep trying to nonetheless. Researchers say it is difficult to accurately assess the impact of TV on children because parents lie about how much their children watch. Your misrepresentations may not be bald-faced, it's just hard to acknowledge the truth. Do the math on how many hours a week your child sits in front of a screen and you'll be convinced that you added wrong. *How can two hours a day add up to fourteen hours a week?* My husband and I are forever spinning the most positive damage assessment. *She's singing along! It teaches the alphabet! It's interactive! She can use the mouse! She loves it! Excellent hand-eye coordination! She's dancing! She's so smart!*

Accept the following as facts: the TV is a surrogate, a surrogate for you and all the things that you aren't presently available to give. TV is resting time; a better place for a child to rest is in a bed. No Einsteins have yet emerged from a childhood under the tutelage of videos, no matter what it says on the package. Children learn from TV, yes, but nearly everything they learn will be too much and too soon. Anything useful that they learn from TV can be taught by you if you will muster the same cleverness and consistency. When you can't, you are the one who turns on the TV, and you are the one who must turn it off. When it is on, ideally you are too. Right at hand, reading the invisible warning rolling like a closed caption across the screen your child is glued to. *Wake up! We are holding your children hostage. If you ever want to see them alive again, turn this off!*

The next time you park your kid in front of the TV, set a timer, knowing the timer is for you. When the timer goes off, step forward and speak. Whatever you say should start with "let's." Let's play. Let's go to the park. Let's read. Let's go outside. Let's cook. Let's blow bubbles. Let's chase. Let's tickle. Let's paint. Let's pick flowers. You can stand on the sidelines bloviating all day about how bad TV is and it won't make a bit of difference. *You* must animate and activate the life you share.

All that being said, it can be truly eye-opening to watch TV with your child. It will affirm, each time, the primacy of your role in your child's life. And it will demonstrate, over and over, that you cannot impose a standard for your child that is any different from the way you, as an adult, live. In that way, you begin to see that the sticky business of discipline begins with yourself.

18

Self-Discipline

DON'T DECEIVE YOURSELF

Zuigan Gen Osho called to himself every day, "Master!" and answered, "Yes, sir!" Then he would say, "Be wide awake!" and answer, "Yes, sir!" "Henceforward, never be deceived by others!" "No, I won't!"

—*Gateless Gate*, case 12

*I*t was on my thigh, the back of my left thigh, where—my daughter's tooth prints pink and pulsing—the subject of discipline first occurred to me. *Ouch!* She was no longer the self-regulating little device she started out as. No longer only benign belly and bowel functions. Somewhere between last night's bath and this morning's diaper, she had transformed into a fanged menace, a horned demon. I reacted at peak throttle. I slapped her arm, hard, and we both crumpled in a flood of fear and tears.

Oh, my. This is going to require more than endless work and ceaseless hours. It will take more than cleanliness, organization, cooking, laundry, and shopping. It will take more than all my money and good intentions. This is going to require the *d* word, dammit: discipline.

There is no topic that piques and polarizes parents more than discipline. How we wish our children would be *good*! And by "good" we mean easy for us. They aren't, not all the time, not one of them. How much we aim to be *good* parents! And by "good" we usually mean different from our own, with different views and means of discipline. We so seldom are, although our children keep coming at us, provoking us to take a wiser approach.

This is a thicket, you know, this business of being bad and being good and how much we indulge and how much we inflict. Add to it the flammability of fatigue, anger, and pride and it is shocking how much of the time we can get it all so terribly wrong.

I was a witness to a visit made by my mother's pastor during her last stay in the hospital. Intending perhaps to lessen the gravity of her circumstance, he wandered lightheartedly into a bit of a sermon on raising kids. He seemed sorry about it, but he also seemed certain: those boys of his needed a wallop nearly every day. Indeed, they forced his hand! My mother, who had spanked me only once growing up and as she did, sobbed at the pain to us both, lay stone-faced in bed. Numbed by her fate and perhaps struck dumb by this message, she offered up nothing. Not a nod. Not one nervous smile. She could never be righteous, but she could be silently, unshakably good.

I think of my mother often—*I think of her now*—as the flash points of parenting come on fast and close. I think of her bawling out loud at the shame and sadness of intentionally hurting her child. Her first time, and she was already so disappointed in herself! When you, too, are brought to tears by your own rage, you will know what I know from my mother, although the wisdom usually comes one wallop too late. You will feel many things after you strike too hard or shriek too loud or otherwise terrify your child, but you will never feel right. The subject of discipline shows you your interdependence; it demonstrates your oneness. When you deliver the blow, you will suffer the impact. The question is, how does it come to this? Better still, how can we stop even one second short of too late?

When babies are little we are told, and then we come to see, that every outburst is a cry for something needed. A few days or weeks into the drill and we can decode the pitch and duration of the wail, look at our watches, and know everything instantly. She's hungry. She's tired. She needs a diaper change. And later, she's teething. She's overstimulated. She's bored. Or, she's sick. All nonjudgmental deductions that trigger our compassion and action. But when our children get a tad older, appearing more sophisticated and encountering a more complicated world, we're likely to ease back on the compassion. We mistake them for fully evolved human beings. Sometimes we mistake them for the enemy. Assaulted by the rude new disguise of their cries for help, we judge them. *You're being bad,* we think. We say it, too, delivered impulsively with a spirited correction to their minds or their bodies.

Now, who's practicing being the good parent?

We are deceiving ourselves anytime we view our children as separate from the conditions that we ourselves still largely create: separate from the circumstances of their environment; separate from the state of their minds, bodies, and bellies; and separate from the monumental influence we as parents impose. We look at them with loathing, these new, inscrutable children, these *other* children. In this shift of perception, we expel our babies from the unity of *we* and engage them in a battle in which they can only get stomped. These are the moments when wakefulness waves its puny white flag. If we can wake up, we will see that we cannot separate self from other. We cannot separate restraint from self-restraint. We cannot separate respect from self-respect. We cannot separate discipline from self-discipline. We cannot separate. We delude ourselves by even *perceiving* someone as separate, and we deceive ourselves with our delusions. There is nothing outside ourselves.

This sounds like Buddhist mumbo jumbo, you might say. Nice in theory but not in practice because of the vagaries of kids' temperaments or genetics or even the influence of the devil. But I don't know anything about those things, and anything I do know doesn't help me handle the moment of impact. When my daughter does something I don't like or can't fathom, something embarrassing or inappropriate, I have to go to work on it immediately, and all I have to work with is myself. Oh, sure, I could try working directly on her. *Let me work my stiff, open palm violently onto your plump behind.* But I don't want to do that! It will be a time much, much later and a climate much, much cooler when I can work with my daughter in other ways—dialogue, compromise, explanation, role play—but for now (maybe forever) all I have to work with is myself.

How? I must slow my reactions down. I must observe the situation and intuit the cause. I must consider her developmental urges and instincts. I must listen, carefully, to her words. I must use my own words, or silence, precisely. I must alter the aggravating situation, often by removing her, sometimes by removing me. I must bring all of my attention and all of my power to correcting what I have done or not done to unwittingly allow, encourage, foster, and fester this mess taking place right now in my own house. And if you argue that this is all too liberal, too permissive, because my daughter must learn what is right and what is wrong, I will respond that in fact my daughter will learn in the same way she learns almost all things—by watching, hearing, and imitating *me*. My child will do what I do and say what I say, but she will never, without coercion, *do* what I *say*. How I wish that every single time she could watch me calm down, cool off, take responsibility, and solve the problem. Only then can she learn to do likewise.

I once read a doctor's advice on dealing with a thumb-sucking problem, which can be a world-class annoyance. Wear a rubber band on your arm, the doctor said, and snap it sharply against your wrist anytime you *think* about hounding your kid to stop sucking his thumb. Discipline seems to work on this principle, too. Turn everything on yourself *first* and then take stock of whatever problems remain. There won't be nearly so many.

Lest you think I'm some kind of born-again peacenik, someone who levitates above the fray, let me assure you that none of these conclusions were reached without pain or punishment to us both, without inflicting the horrors of rough handling when I was simply too frustrated or stubborn to take a breather. I lose it all the time. We all lose it all the time. The point is not that we lose our cool, the point is how quickly we find it again.

About the time I realized dismally that I had no disciplinary method, no philosophy, and no higher authority, messianic messages began appearing. Perhaps this is how mine will appear for you.

A book tipped me off that most tantrums occur at moments of low blood sugar or fatigue. Aha! Discipline yourself to live strictly by routine. Offer precisely timed meals, snacks, and naps and you can preempt some of those nasty scenes. You can quite nearly prevent tantrums in public when you discipline yourself to avoid lengthy or ill-timed shopping trips.

An expert on daytime TV said out-of-bounds behavior is a cry for attention. As doses of high-intensity attention, punishments can reinforce inappropriate behavior. Next time, *withdraw* your attention and see how quickly the behavior self-corrects. Announce your intention to leave the room until the tantrum is over. Then leave the room. Abandon the fight. Ignore the offender. Let the fire go out, as a fire always does if you have the self-discipline to stop fueling it. After that, rally yourself to provide positive forms of attention. Play, read, draw, tumble, and frolic. Together.

There are situations that simply scream out for your decisive intervention—circumstances that require you to cut through the behavior before the both of you spiral further into chaos. When Georgia began having tantrums, the curative was often, "Go to your room." We were stunned when it worked, but it usually did. If your child defies the order, then discipline yourself and take refuge in *your* room. For this, I designated a cushy reading chair in my bedroom, where I hardly ever had the luxury to sit anymore. This became mom's "quiet chair," where I parked myself to decelerate conflicts. Invariably, my tamed two-year-old would venture in within minutes to make up with hugs and kisses. Your child, after all, wants something, and what he or she usually wants is your love.

It's funny how many discipline problems occur around the very things we haven't—*ahem*—been very disciplined about ourselves. Face up to whatever lack of discipline you've forgiven in yourself, because you're about to propagate it in every single generation that succeeds you. Are you disorganized, messy, hot tempered, foulmouthed, lazy, or forgetful? Fix it. Want your child to eat better? Then add variety, balance, healthfulness, and regularity to your own diet. Are you expecting her to eat her meals at the table? Where do you eat yours? Having a hard time getting your child to brush her teeth? When's the last time she saw you brush yours, or even helped? Bathing is a battle? Then get into the tub and have fun. How can you get your child to sleep at a decent hour? Go to bed on time. Establish a routine for yourselves and administer it every single day and night. Seeking the surety of a governable household and the sanity of consistent behavior? Be firm with yourself: tell your child what you expect, give clear instructions, and impose consistent limits. Over and over and over again. Want your child to learn to handle difficult emotions and overcome fears? Then do likewise. Express yourself calmly, own up to your feelings, and don't be afraid to be honest. If you don't believe you have the capacity to administer your child's welfare, he or she won't believe it either. Want your child to be *good*? Then *be* good.

One of the fastest ways to become a wise parent is to remember what you used to know so well: that children act up when they are hungry, tired, or uncomfortable. It remains true for them, as it does for us, long past the point when we can recognize it. These are still the easy days, after all. Our children are still little. My mother used to quote her own mother when she tried to help me put all of this into perspective: "When children are little, they have little problems." When children are big, we'll worry about that later.

"We do not bite." I hold my daughter eye to eye and say emphatically to us both. It is a promise to her and a reminder to me to keep my own sharp teeth and swift hands to myself, to silence my shaming words, to revive my flagging attention, and to restore my faith in boundless, compassionate love above all.

No matter what the situation, how perplexing or intolerable, you always have a starting point when you start with yourself. *Yes, sir!*

19

Magic Words

LEARNING TO TALK

All evil karma ever committed by me since of old.
On account of my beginningless greed, anger and
  ignorance.
Born of my body, mouth and thought. Now I atone
  for it all.

—Verse of Atonement

I stared at the take-home letter from my daughter's preschool teacher. It dealt with conflict resolution, or the
indelicate fact that outside of our arms, our children were likely
to claw and kick one another.

"We don't emphasize saying 'I'm sorry' until children are
able to have a conceptual understanding of what it means," the
letter read. To me, that was lunacy. I'd learned a little magic in my
two years as a mother, and the magic was this: I'm sorry.

In no other relationship had I seen, really seen, the ruin that
could be wrought by my own attitude, the trembling and awe I

could produce by a loosened yell, a door slam, or an angry face. No other relationship had the precarious proximity my daughter and I shared. I couldn't predict precisely when a wayward push would break the last thread of my restraint, but I could predict that it would happen. We each have our breaking points. When I breached mine, I bore witness to its savage aftermath. My daughter's spirit imploded. Her sense of security was crushed.

And thus began my need to run, indeed race, to the instant healing and restoration magically granted by the utterance "I'm sorry." I couldn't very well teach her to use those words unless I had familiar access to them myself, and I was sorely out of practice.

At some point in our lives, "I'm sorry" becomes a very difficult thing to say (perhaps at the point we have a conceptual understanding of the words). The weight of its responsibility seems too heavy, the admission too severe, the losing, yes the losing, is too dear. We engineer other ways to say it, appended with other words to ease its bearing or divert its meaning. We want peace on our terms, you see. We want to keep our supremacy intact. We want to end the battle by *winning,* not by ending. These contrivances begin, "I'm sorry, but . . ." After the "but" comes self-defense and justification, explanation and blame, a fist in a glove. Then there is the imperial "I'm sorry that you feel that way." There is no sorry in this kind of sorry, and we know it, but that's the kind of sorry that we trade in. No wonder hostilities never cease.

It had been a long time since I had said, simply, "I'm sorry," and let the silence afterward enfold and erase the harm done. But I begin to do it now, because my need to undo is urgent and unquestioned. "I'm sorry," I say, when I've buckled and the sky has fallen. "I'm sorry," I say to someone who has no conceptual understanding of the words. "I'm sorry," I say to myself. And, miraculously, the world is made right again. The whole world, the only world my daughter and I live in, the fifteen hundred square feet that composes our universe. She holds no grudges; she doesn't know how. When I say I'm sorry, we can begin anew, awash in love and tenderness toward each other.

These two little words *I'm sorry* show me everything about myself. They show me how attached I am to my hurts and grievances. How stingy I am with my whole heart. How seldom I mean what I say. How simple it is to achieve peace. True peace, unconditional peace. In reality, peace is always right here—everything getting along just fine, thank you—until I exile myself with my anger and self-centeredness, my ignorant perception that *I*, the innocent party, am separate from *you*, the egregious offender. In this case, the egregious offender in the purple tutu and bunny ears with a finger up her nose. (If I could stop still long enough to see, really see, what is in front of me instead of dwelling on the bleak landscape in my head, I could easily erupt into laughter instead of anger, and that would be the end of it.)

Saying you're sorry is a rather miraculous act of atonement, and all the great religions talk up atonement. There must be something there, but what is it? Atonement means reconciliation or reparation. Maezumi Roshi, who found wisdom on every page of *Webster's*, used to marvel at the very appearance of the word, because there, hidden in plain sight, is the whole enchilada: at-one-ment. Being one with everything. Unified. Harmonious. Being sorry, truly sorry, closes the gap that has grown wide between you and your beloved. The gap doesn't really exist, but when you think it does, it does. This is your new spiritual practice: saying "I'm sorry." Say "I'm sorry" and let the pure power of your intention put the world back in one piece. It works, and you can tell. There is always a feeling of reunion after you do this; there is a feeling of coming home.

I'm learning to apologize without any regard for whether I'm first or last, right or wrong. Sometimes it seems that all I ever do is make amends. That's okay. Every time I do, it has a better outcome than all the times I don't.

But there's more I need to learn, because words—chosen carefully, spoken calmly—help me recognize and release feelings that otherwise intensify. I practice pausing, breathing, and saying, "I'm angry right now." Or "I'm frustrated right now." Or "I'm sad right now." *How did I get this far along without ever being free to say these things?* In nursery school they call this "using your words." I'm well into my forties and just now cracking into the pre-K curriculum! When I speak a feeling, it changes me, it changes my body, it loosens the noose and lowers the temperature. It clarifies the situation for me and for everyone around me. Outbursts are allayed. Spoken, these words by themselves are safe, but unspoken, they smolder into fire and brimstone.

I am also discerning what little *needs* to be said. Any word that causes hurt, any word that degrades, any word that poisons the pristine air, is better left in your mouth, dissolving on your tongue so you can taste your own bitter brew. What power there is in these gusts, and we alone have the power to release or retain. This is mental training. This is meditation. These revelations take time to surface, which they do when I learn to give *myself* a time-out, retreating to the calm of a "quiet chair" in my bedroom. This backward step becomes something I do a lot. Soon, when my daughter happens to see me, sitting silently in my bedroom chair, she proffers apology on her own. She knows for herself when the world is out of whack, and she now has the means to make it right.

I know there are people—because I know it in me—who cannot push themselves past the chasm. Saying "I'm sorry" to anyone, least of all their child, is impossible. They live in a labyrinth of twisted logic, imprisoned by the high walls of hierarchy. Behind this defense they are not strong; they are wobbly and weak. To them I say: *I'm sorry.* Master Dogen tells us, "Kind speech has the power to turn the destiny of a nation." That is not wimpy.

Even as I'm learning about myself, my daughter is learning that she, too, has the strength to take responsibility and the means to change the world.

Words are magic. All words are, not just *please* and *thank you.* The words my daughter will use are the ones she hears; the words I want her to use she must hear from me. So when I'm alarmed by her annoying use of the imperative, her bossy instructions to me without the sweetening of a "please," I listen to myself for a while. How much of what I say to her is a curt command? Nearly all of it.

How would I have her speak? With all the subtlety, compassion, kindness, and power that is in my own magical vocabulary, when I learn to talk.

PART FOUR

Waking Up

TURN THE LIGHT INWARD

20

No Trace

THEY GROW UP SOON ENOUGH

Form is no other than emptiness, emptiness no other
  than form;
Form is exactly emptiness, emptiness exactly form;
Sensation, conception, discrimination, awareness are
  likewise like this.

—*Heart Sutra*

*F*orm is emptiness," Buddhism teaches. "And emptiness
is form." What could it possibly mean? It means this: it
means I cried on the night of Georgia's first birthday.

The bakery cake was ugly. She bawled in bewilderment at
the crowd around the table. The presents didn't interest her. She
fled my arms to the cuddles of her babysitter. My humiliation
was complete, but it was something else that brought me to tears.
It was the finality. My baby was done with her first year. And de-
spite my hurry, I was not. I had chosen this night to box up her
baby clothes, refolding the tiny come-home things, sobbing at

the poop and spit-up stains. They were already relics. How could it be over?

People will tell you so many things, passing on their hindsight and regrets. *Love them when they are little. Cherish the early days.* I would say it all again, but I'm not sure you can hear it until you reach the other side, open your eyes, and let the tears of recognition come. There is not one piece of life that you can grasp, contain, or keep, not even the life you created and hold right now in your arms. I confess I never tried to slow it down, ever pushing forward to some imagined place of competence for me and independence for her. On this night, though, I could see how fast it all would go. How fast, how sad. Every happy day brimming with bittersweetness.

This is how it passes: no matter where we are we think of someplace else. The place after nighttime feedings, the place beyond twelve-a-day diapers, the certain bliss that beckons from a distant shore. This is how we spend our lives; this is how we spend *their* lives, motoring past milestones as if collecting so many merit badges.

We can be forgiven for this tendency, in part, because childhood is full of tests and measures, percentiles and comparisons. Bring your baby to the doctor's office and the nurse will plot her as a dot on a growth chart. I inscribed these glyphs dutifully on my calendar—how many pounds now, how many inches now—satisfied that we were safely on course to get somewhere. Where is that somewhere? Where is that place that I can relax the tension on the wheel, ease off the accelerator?

Not one bit of life is a weight or a measure, a list or a date, a tick or a tock. It is never a result or an outcome. What it is is a continual marvel, a wondrous flow without distance or gap, a perpetual stream in which we bob and float. We are buffered from nothing and yet never quite fully immersed because our thinking mind keeps eyeing the banks, gauging the current, scoping for landmarks, and striving for some kind of perfect, elusive destination. There isn't a destination. Life keeps going. It keeps going within us; when we're not attentive, it keeps going without us.

Treat this as a race and you will get ahead of yourself. Life has its own perpetual motion, and yet we think we need to rev the engine. *What can I do,* you will think, *to get her to eat more cry less sleep all night take solids roll over sit up start crawling wave bye-bye start walking stop falling hold a cup start talking feed herself start playgroup potty train eat more cry less sleep all night start preschool make friends share toys run hop ride a bike draw write read use prepositions eat more cry less sleep all night?* And if there's nothing I can do to make it happen sooner, why is that kid over there doing it already?

There is a compartment above our hall closet, a compartment that is never opened. Inside is our daughter's bouncer chair. A bouncer chair is a kind of rocking sling that will serve you for a sliver of time that is dense with sentiment and yet for me now is completely indistinguishable and forgotten. I cannot recall when in her first year she outgrew her chair, but she did, and apparently we didn't. Many, many things from her past have been handed down or sold, but this one was too important to her parents. We made a special point of putting it in a special place where we will keep it forever and never see it again. What you keep does not keep. Form is emptiness.

But how valiantly we try to seize it! Freeze it! Say cheese it! Entire industries depend on this urge to have something to show for these lives of ours. Like all first-time parents, we were customers of the year at our corner 1-Hour Photo, snapping seventy-two frames every week and waving them around to a numbed collective. True, every photo is a priceless original. The moment will never come this way again. Eventually, even *you* succumb to the limits of interest, the futility of the record, the pallor of memory, and the ceaselessness of the march.

Perhaps it is because we realize that we can keep nothing that we try to keep something. When Georgia was three, she willingly disposed of her two surviving pacifiers. Oh happy day! In our home—and I would suggest in nearly every home of a binky-loving three-year-old—these little nibs were reviled by mom and dad. They were the subject of daily negotiations and repudiations. We were deeply worried about her teeth and her palette; we worried at least as much about what others would think. We tried one thing, we tried another in the tug of war to extricate them. Then, like everything else, Georgia did it herself when she was ready. That night she told her daddy matter-of-factly, "I put my binkies in the trash today." Later I caught him groping in the garbage up to his armpit to reclaim the grisly keepsakes. What lasts forever does not last. Emptiness is form.

We hurry up our children only to try, in vain, to hold a part of them back. Everything happens in its own time soon enough. Soon enough is always too soon.

"Don't push the river," my Zen teacher says to pull me back when he sees my mind wander off in search of a someday. "Let the future come to you." Ready or not, it does. It toddles forward on its first step, teeters on a threshold for one agonizing instant, then turns and waves bye-bye. Good-bye, sweet baby; hello, sweet girl.

When I occupy that instant, any instant, my heart's fullness reminds me that *here* is everything and everything is *here*. This is how I would live if I had mastery of myself—without wasting one sideways glance at what was or what has yet to be.

I put away the clothes that night as I would again on many other nights. My girl was a big girl, her own girl, with her own loves and her own life. I was a spectator, but the show was splendid and I still had the best seat in the house. If I were forever looking forward or lingering too long looking backward, I would miss too much. I would miss it all.

21

No Separation

THE REALITY OF SAYING BYE-BYE

The moon above the clouds is ever the same;
Valleys and mountains are separate from each other.
All are blessed, all are blessed;
Are they one or are they two?

—*Gateless Gate*, case 35

The hardest day is not the day the doctor comes at your tender two-month-old with a needle, or the thirty-odd times you will repeat the terror to complete the vaccination scorecard.

The hardest day is not the day that you rise from all shaky fours with a tiny tooth torn from a bloody gum, the day you race into futility with the dire hope that dentistry can restore the pearly perfection of "before."

The hardest day is not the day that you sop up vomit from the leather seat, poop from a cashmere coat, or pee from a puddle two steps shy of the airplane potty. The last of these, at least, is sterile on arrival.

The hardest day is the day you say good-bye. For many of us right away and for all of us eventually, this is every day. Saying good-bye is the hardest thing to do. The thing we must do the most is the thing we care to do the least, and so it keeps coming around the bend. It is, in the end, life's only lesson.

It can be quite comic, at least in the telling.

Back when Georgia was just ten weeks old, we lobbied my sister to fly in for the weekend so the stir-crazed two of us (remember when it was just "the two of us"?) could have our first night out as mom and dad. We huddled in our awkward, altered state in the movie theater, jumpy with the brazen lawlessness of leaving the cell phone turned on. The movie rolled, we squirmed, we rustled, we tried, and then we whispered to each other the surprise ending to this half-hearted excursion: *Ready to go home?* Forty-five minutes after peeling out of the house, we hurried in again, nuzzling the baby back in our arms. There was too much love for the leaving.

Intermittently, our motivation for exodus would mount, and we would try to say good-bye again. The saga of finding, keeping, losing, and weeping over babysitters can be a simmering subtext in your life. For mothers, finding a sitter is a nuanced blend of desperate need, blind faith, gut instinct, and overpowering guilt, delicately seasoned by a sense of your child's developmental readiness and emotional well-being. For fathers, it can be rather more straightforward: *Let's get a sitter Saturday night.* Even when everything clicked—the baby was well, happy, and bonded with a person she loved; the babysitter was available, competent, caring, and only minimally tattooed—there still loomed what could always be a long and yawning moment, the screeching, squalling, bloody-murder moment of saying good-bye. These were the hardest times: when we had to say good-bye, turn away, and close the door as if stealing away from the scene of a crime.

We skulked to the car, where we trembled and held hands, emboldening each other to back out of the driveway.

In its alternating forms and varying degrees, this is the substance of what psychologists call separation anxiety, the fear felt by your baby, then your toddler, then your child, when you leave. Not to mention the equal fear you feel as well. For all the wishing that *your child* would grow out of it and get over it and get on with it, separation is not a one-sided anxiety. We do it alone and yet we do it together. We disappear from each other's sight! And then what happens? Tell me: what happens to you when you are out of my sight? What happens when you are gone?

In one way, nothing comes out of this question, because you'll never know the answer. We may think we know, but we cannot know what happens outside our line of vision. In another way, everything comes out of this question because, by not knowing, we must cultivate trust and demonstrate faith. A life of faith is a very long time in the learning, but most of us have all the time it takes.

Georgia had several beloved caregivers in her infancy. Our home was blessed. In succession, her part-time nannies helped me find solitude and strength, gave me the time to work and work out, and steadied our home life when it was listing to port. *More hands on deck, mom overboard!* These were sweet and sensitive women; they were like sisters and friends; and most important, they loved my daughter madly and she them. But still we fumbled at the parting, Georgia and I. Some days had good starts and many did not. Bad starts were ruinous. Authorities tell us that this hullabaloo is because our babies have not yet devised the mental trickery of "object constancy," or the ability to hold an image of a departed object in their minds. If they only knew the images I held in *my* mind after I walked away from her sobs. I

carried my guilt and dread like my own hulking carcass until I
could see my daughter's bright, happy face again.

Oh, there were reassurances:

Your mommy will be right back!

She only cried a minute!

These things might often be true, but they were such flimsy,
tissue-paper sails to ferry us through the dark distance of *being
gone.*

Our difficulty with separating would dog my daughter and
me nearly all the days of her toddlerhood. The stiffening in my
spine as we approach her school most mornings tells me that
perhaps it still does.

We have always found trusty helpers to lend their understanding, even when Georgia and I still could not swing the gap.
When Georgia was one, I had the economical idea of enrolling
her in day care two days a week. I could do more work and spend
less of the proceeds on child care. That was the idea. The imple-
mentation was awful. When I picked her up after making her
first day's sneaky good-bye, she looked woebegone and bedraggled in nothing but a diaper and dirt, dazed with betrayal, hardly
recognizing and then hardly believing that her mom had stepped
out of the eternal sunshine to reclaim her. "She had a good day,"
the teachers chimed as I staggered in and out. "She looks like
she's been living under a bridge!" I wailed to my husband when
we got home. This was not what you would call your best foot
forward. None of the rest of the days were easy. But they were
short in number. I pulled her out of the program within three
months and kept her at home, where I thought love meant never
having to say good-bye. If only it did.

There were other departures afoot. There always are. As her
illness allowed, my mother made visits. Her prognosis was not yet

final, but the percentages were grim. On each of a half-dozen trips, her here and us there, we might have had a hysterical parting, but we didn't, even though we never knew what crying shame could befall us next. *Tell me: what happens to you when you are out of my sight? What happens when you are gone?* Perhaps my mother was teaching me then, as she is teaching me still in this recollection, how to step forward and take leave. Be calm and confident in separating, because even in separation there is no separation, and the trust you impart will be the trust with which your child carries on.

When Georgia was two, she and I spent four afternoons a week at a preschool where the focus of the curriculum for her age group was to learn separation. That meant that over nine months we made more than 140 attempts to say good-bye. *I'll be right back! Have a good time! See you later!* The training period was not long enough for us. I spent the better part of a year pounding pancakes at the Play-Doh table rather than take a leap into the beyond. Along the way, I heard the most profound advice. All of it affirmed the mutuality of our experience:

She takes her cues from you.

She wants you to see how much she loves you.

Establish a routine so she'll know what to expect every day.

Later I wondered: were they talking about me or her? In the doing, there is no way to separate the two. In the doubting, we stand a world apart.

On her last trip to see us, I drove my mother to the airport and waited at the gate until the boarding began. We hugged and kissed. She took her ticket and held her place in line, face forward, shoulder bag hoisted, inching ahead until she crossed over to the vanishing point. She did not look back at me. She did not buckle and break. She looked for all the world like any other passenger making any other trip. Only she and I knew that hers was a jet plane to heaven.

A few months later, when all the treatments and diagnoses were done, she uttered a mother's eternal wonder, "I don't know how you can live without me." There it was finally. She just didn't know. I just don't know. We just don't know. We carry on, coming and going, into the inconceivable. This is how we live in faith—faith not in what we claim to know but in what we never will.

Everything, even a melodrama, ends. Leaving the things you love is one of life's essential tasks, and so we all find a way to do it. How could it be otherwise? There will be happy, silly, carefree good-byes. And there will be painful ones. In the end, whether you are leaving a room or leaving the house, whether you are closing a door or closing your eyes, there comes the time to simply say good-bye.

22

Right Now

ATTENTION, MOM!
CAN YOU HANDLE IT RIGHT NOW?

Be aware of where you really are twenty-four hours a day. You must be most attentive. When nothing at all gets on your mind, it all merges harmoniously, without boundaries—the whole thing is empty and still, and there is no more doubt or hesitation in anything you do.

—Yuanwu

Your infant screams it. Your toddler throws it. Your preschooler demands it. Each is a call for attention now, now, now.

Do you aspire to live in the moment? It always sounds like the place you want to be. Then go ahead, start with this one right now: when your inconsolable infant is mired in a colicky squall. When your two-year-old crashes past his flimsy limits into the bottomless terror of a tantrum. When your four-year-old is jackhammering "Mommy! Mommy! Mommy!" into your cranium.

All the careful preparations and good intentions you bring to the job of motherhood come down to this: can you handle it right now? The now that is noisy, exhausted, messy, sick, late, sad, exasperated, and above all, bored? Excuse me; I'm still waiting for the *other* now, that quiet and contented one. It will show up, eventually. Children do stop crying. Mothers do too. Children go to sleep. A good while later, you will too. In the interim, worlds collide.

In the company of my child, I realize how much time I spend in some other place entirely. Indeed, how much of my life I spend in the reverie of my own thoughts and schemes. Her laughs and cries, her outbursts and calls, snap me back to where we are right now. Can I manage to stay here for a little while longer before I compulsively trail off again? It's very hard to do. In my bleakest times, one more plea from her hooks me, and I thrash back, as if fighting for my life. I'm not really fighting for my life; I'm fighting for *my way* of life. Namely, the lost luxury of solitude combined with unlimited escapes into e-mail and the Internet.

I know that all my daughter wants is for me to be present at every fresh, new moment of her life. How sad that I can't give her that. My exits are so habitually ingrained that I'm no longer sure how much of my own life I've shown up for.

Even my efficiency as a caregiver, I come to realize, stems from my inability to stay put. *Let's power through this feeding to get onto the nap. Let's get this nap started so I can go on to something else. Sorry, sorry, can't come now; I'm making tomorrow's lunch.* I rev along on restlessness, on to the next, next, next thing in endless chase. With me at the controls, days turn to dust. Yes, I know there is much to do, but there is enough to do right here without dreaming up something else to worry about.

A friend confides that she can hardly tolerate time spent

playing with her toddler. "As soon as I get down on the floor, my mind races, my heart jumps. I can't stand it." This from a woman who has just quit her job to spend more time with her child. We all want more time with our precious children; it's just hardly ever the time right now. The problem is, right now is the only time it ever is.

When my daughter was three, I joined a dozen other parents one night at an orientation for her school's prekindergarten program, which awaited her in the fall. The classroom walls were adorned with the figurative drawings and scrawled writings of the current crop of four-year-olds. We parents eyed them approvingly, evidence of the early literacy skills we couldn't wait to witness in our own budding geniuses. A mother raised her hand.

"I see that some of the kids can write their names. Is preparing them for kindergarten part of your curriculum?" We all shared her eagerness.

"We do not prepare them for anything," the teacher said, with the full force of her convictions. "If your child is ready to write, we support them. If your child isn't ready to write, we support them. Our job is to support your child wherever he or she is *right now.*" Her answer pierced me with its correctness. Inside I sobbed. *This is where my child belongs.*

I look at my daughter's open and shining face. In her mind there are no old jobs, old hurts, or old grudges. No gossip or fretting. Not the debris of dashed hopes or unrealized plans. Nothing hounding her. Nothing to prove. No list on the refrigerator. There is just immediacy, honesty, and perfection. Somehow she trusts that everything she needs will be provided here and now. If I could muster just a tiny bit of her colossal faith that everything is, and will be, okay, I could live differently.

Maybe later.

23

Fresh Start

ALWAYS JUST BEGINNING

You may suppose that time is only passing away and not understand that time never arrives.

—Dogen Zenji, "The Time-Being"

*A*gain, again, again!"
There is a saying about life: you don't get a second chance. Your child is here to tell you otherwise. You get a lot of second chances. You get a lot of third chances. You get many fourth chances. Before all is said and done, you get about a million chances to do things that you never wanted to do even once. You will do many things again, so many times again: knocking down the same old blocks, pushing the same old swing, reading the same old story, singing the same old song, winding the same old wind-up to its predictable ending. Predictable to you, that is, same old, same old you.

Children learn by repetition. And by their repetition we can learn too. We can learn how cynical we are, how busy and easily bored, how impatient and restless. Those are the things we can see in ourselves many times a day. It can take far longer—a lifetime—for us to realize what they, with their brilliantly open minds, still see quite plainly: nothing, absolutely nothing repeats. Every moment of this life is altogether new. They do things again and again because they haven't yet calculated the probabilities; they haven't yet anticipated the ending. They are still doing what we have ceased to do: see the infinite possibilities. They are not yet cutting life short by their jaded cleverness. "Been there, done that," we say, as we dispose of our unrealized potential.

It is impossible to conceive of the true, dynamic nature of life. It is ever flowing, never arriving at the same place twice, indeed, never even pausing to arrive. And yet we think we've seen it all.

Maezumi Roshi was fascinated with the phenomenon of life as it really is. He frequently referred to a portion of the *Abhidharma Sutra* in which Buddha taught that in one day our life is born and dies more than six billion times. "More than six billion times!" he would exclaim, like a child delighted with a new toy. If you listened to his talks then, or if you read them now, you hear him return to this point again and again and again. It never bored him. Of course, every time he uttered it was a new discovery; it was not the same old, same old thing at all.

We can acknowledge this truth just by facing the scientific fact of our existence. Every instant, cells in our body are changing: they die, they regenerate. The earth spins. Air moves. Grass grows. Every moment is a beginning and an end. Nothing is fixed but our fixations. We affix on our habitual views; we affix on our habitual behaviors. And we think we're done.

What's next? Where to? Anxiety lurks.

What looks like repetition is practice. In one eternal stretch, my daughter took the same turkey-on-white-bread lunch to pre-K for eighty-two days straight. She was practicing eating her lunch. She wore the same grungy pink sandals. She was practicing choosing her shoes. She tore straightaway to the swings as soon as we arrived at school each morning. She was practicing pumping her legs. Look how serenely I now feign my acceptance of these inexplicable ruts! What I thought at the time was, *How can I move her on to wheat? How can I get her to wear tennis shoes? How can I entice her to pick up a pencil?*

This is how life comes to us: over and over again, so we can refresh ourselves into open-mindedness, so we can practice being alive. Another chance to let it go, another chance to let it be, another chance to see how it goes this time. How sweet that our children keep bonking us awake with such tiny, white-bread offenses.

Here it comes again: another start of another day. What a reprieve! You have incalculable chances to change the ending. To change your attitude. To be the new you. Whether you know it or not, you already are the new you. Forget what you think, lose the foregone conclusion, and just be new.

24

Be Yourself

YOU'RE NOT WHO YOU THINK YOU ARE

Ummon said to the assembled monks, "Between heaven and earth, within the universe, there is one treasure. It is hidden in the mountain form. You take the lantern, entering the Buddha hall, and take the temple gate, placing it above the lantern!"

—*Blue Cliff Record*, case 62

Why abandon the seat in your own home to wander in vain through the dusty regions of another land?

—Dogen Zenji, "Principles of Seated Meditation"

*M*ommy," said my daughter, "you be the witch." She was already cavorting around the front yard as the imperiled princess.

"Okay," I said drearily, thinking: *How long am I going to have to do this?*

"No, Mommy," she corrected, "you be the witch."

"Okay," I said again, louder. *What's her problem now?*

"No, Mommy!" She stomped her foot, furious at my ignorance. "You beeeeeee the witch!" I looked at her for one bewildered second before her words whacked me over the head and I had a sudden realization.

"Okay," I cackled, now dripping with menace, curling my hands into claws, and setting off in pursuit. *So this is what it means to* be.

Children are exemplars of the art of being. Wherever they are, they are completely immersed: in mud, in make-believe, in laughter, in tears, or in spaghetti sauce up to their eyeballs. Without a bit of self-consciousness, they lose themselves in what they *are;* they literally throw themselves away. This is the kind of losing in which everything is found.

We, on the other hand, rarely lose ourselves in activity, but we are plenty lost nonetheless. We lose ourselves in mental distractions; we disconnect our words from our actions. Caught up in our own nonstop internal commentary, we confuse what is happening in our heads with what is really happening. We habitually choose to do this because our thoughts seem to be so much more entertaining, elevating, urgent, and important than what is occurring in front of us. I didn't want to play in her make-believe because I was too busy concocting my own. Leave it to an intractable preschooler to point out what was obvious except to me: *thinking* is not at all the same as *being*.

I bring this up for consideration should you enter a season of discontent, a season that might well last far beyond four seasons and into the foreseeable future. This is the season in which, with your child reasonably independent, you begin to think that you should come out of this dormancy into someplace else, doing something else, achieving something else, fulfilling something else, transforming into someone else, doing anything but being the witch—*again!*—in the front yard at four o'clock in what might have been the illustrious prime of your life. We all engage in this kind of storytelling, but it is a shame that it preoccupies us when we have so scarcely occupied the life we have.

I should find a job, I've thought.

I should go back to school, I've thought.

I should be a teacher, I've thought.

I should sell real estate, I've thought.

I should write a book, I've thought.

I should be further along in my practice, I've thought.

I don't know where I was when I had these thoughts, but wherever I was, I wasn't altogether there.

We prize our thinking in a way that we value nothing else about our existence, and in so doing we think that without our thoughts we would surely cease to be. We exist when we are thinking just as we exist when we are not thinking—we just aren't aware of it, and in that gulf, all is lost.

We mistakenly think everything is produced by thought, when in fact thinking only produces more thinking! What you really accomplish in your day you do almost entirely without thinking: breathing, digesting, standing, moving about, writing, driving, scratching your head, speaking, sorting laundry, screaming, sweeping floors, making dinner from limp celery and garbanzo beans, sewing miniature mermaid fins from a turquoise sock. Untold, countless, miraculous, and utterly unfathomable deeds. I bet you never thought about it that way. Please, don't start now!

We don't think about the things we do—at least not the things we do well. We think about what we wish we were doing.

I should be more loving.

I should be more disciplined.

I should be stronger.

I should be more patient.

I should be calmer.

I should be wiser.

For certain, we all *thought* we wanted to be mothers and no doubt spend considerable time pondering the complexities of motherhood now, but can we just *be* the mom? Ceaseless think ing obscures us from ourselves the way clouds hide a mountain. We wish we could be some other kind of person, some better kind of mom, and yet we spend so little time in our own undistracted company that we don't really know who we are to begin with.

Maezumi Roshi used to say, "Beneath your robes, do you know who you are?" Underneath the superficialities of appearances, identity, and the arbitrary definitions and preferences that confine us, do you know who you really are? Your power and magnitude? Your generosity and grace? We know ourselves so little that we frequently surprise ourselves. On those good days when you find an extra dose of patience, energy, or attentiveness, where do you suppose those gifts come from? Surely not from outside you. Not from a pastor or teacher. Not from a TV guru. Not from a book, not even this one! On bad days we might even sense our larger, obscured capacity. "I'm not quite myself," we might acknowledge. Then who are you? This question is worth illuminating for yourself, but to do that, you have to turn the light inward. And for the light to reach any depth at all, you have to stop thinking so much.

Relax. It is simpler than it sounds and does not cause seizures.

Thinking is not required to sustain life. Breathing is. That is why, a long time ago, way-seeking people began to use breathing as a tool to liberate the mind from the shackles of thought. They realized how consciously and repetitively focusing on the breath settled the mind from its restless wandering. They saw how this technique could lengthen the space between one thought and the next. They saw the benefits of doing so. You can, too, by using the meditation instructions described at the back of this book. But there's no sense waiting. Time is wasting. Here's a shortcut so you can try it for yourself right now while you're here.

To start, exhale completely. On your next inhalation, silently count "one." When you exhale, silently count "two." Inhale counting "three." Count each exhalation and inhalation up to ten and then start back at one. If you lose the count, begin again at one. If a thought comes up, try not to chase it, and after a while, your thoughts won't chase you either.

That's it? That's it. Ten breaths of your pure being, focused and authentic. Ten breaths in which you fully occupy your own life. Ten breaths of being nothing but you. A ten-breath glimpse of the hidden treasure. It doesn't sound like very long, but it is far longer than you would have had otherwise. Counting your breath is classic meditative practice. You can do it anywhere, while you're doing anything. Anything but thinking.

This is the best way to take care of your family: not to abandon them but to abandon your anxieties, preoccupations, and self-centered distractions. When I find the time to focus on myself in meditation, I find far more time to give to the ones I love, because the self I reveal is selfless.

Dogen Zenji summed up all of Buddhism when he wrote, "To study the Way is to study the self. To study the self is to forget the self."

When you uncover more of your true being through this kind of study, you settle down, but you do not in any way settle for less. You settle for more. By your silent attention and steady practice, you awaken more of your natural generosity, self-discipline, strength, patience, equilibrium, and wisdom. The more you do this, the more you see that this widening space, this quiet passageway, is the door through which everything comes: your satisfaction and peace, your natural attributes, and your higher calling. Every next thing comes right to you without your ruminating or obsessing. It always has. But you are far more likely to notice it this way. When the call or the sign or the itch comes, you can be a real estate agent. Honestly, you can be anything. In fact, you already are.

In the meantime, somebody has to be the witch. Somebody has to be you, and it's never too late to begin.

I stalked enchanted squeals into the long shadows on the summer lawn and we called it a very good day.

PART FIVE

Home Again

EVERY DAY IS A GOOD DAY

25

You'll Know

KNOWING NOTHING IS
KNOWING EVERYTHING

The more you talk and think about it,
the further you wander from the truth.
So cease attachment to talking and thinking
and there is nothing you will not be able to know.

—Seng-t'san, "Verses on the Faith-Mind"

*T*here comes a point when you stop reading the books
and resign yourself to what you don't know. This is precisely how you come to know it all.

When a single, stray cough in the middle of the night tells
you that a cold is coming in the next twenty-four hours: nobody
tells you, but you know.

When your child says her teeth hurt and you instantly suspect an ear infection: it seems farfetched, but you know.

When a thunderburst of tears quashes the thrum of a harried

morning and you cancel the teleconference, stay in your pajamas, cuddle on the rug, and say, "Let's play": it's because you know.

The power of intuition moves through a mother like a silent and gathering storm, amassing such potency, such precision, that when you stop searching elsewhere for the answers, they begin to appear in certitude before you. These are not always the answers that you want—and to that degree you might overlook them in hopeful confusion. But they are sufficient to correct your direction if you trust your eyes, ears, and gut.

When I first began to explore the matter of a nursery school, research led me to a sturdy bungalow on a tidy street where a gaggle of two- to four-year-olds spent the day immersed in the Montessori method. After a solo visit, I was dizzy with ambition to see my daughter enrolled. The children seemed so smart, so quiet, so disciplined, and so very clean. *This is how I want my daughter to turn out!* I filled out the paperwork and scheduled a cursory follow-up visit with the applicant in tow. We arrived for the morning playtime, and Georgia raced onto the cramped, concrete yard at the rear of the school. She struggled up the too high ladder to the too steep slide, flew down too fast and crashed onto the too hard pavement, tearing ugly scuffs on her hands and knees. I carried her crying to the car. My idea of a good place for her was not a good place for her. I didn't have to know it to know it.

This kind of knowing isn't based on the considerable body of knowledge we spend scrupulous days and nights assembling. Of course, it's nice to console ourselves with our carefully drawn conclusions about how to arrive at the *ideal* pregnancy, the *best* birthing method, the *preeminent* pediatrician, the *top* sensory stimulating toys, the *correct* foods, the *fantastic* nanny, the *most excellent* nursery school leading to the *ultimate* kindergarten, and all the right decisions before and after.

We get it into our heads and we take it to heart: what you do today affects the outcome tomorrow. That is the karmic fact of life, and it is abundantly obvious. One thing leads to another. The problem is, we usually try to make the equation work in reverse. We try to make it work *for* us. We approach life not facing forward from where we are but working backward from the ideal outcome we have in mind. We bring to this endeavor all of our intellectual powers and our colossal force of will. Still, how difficult; indeed, how impossible. We do not pilot our cars through the rearview mirror, mightily wishing that we could figure out how to maneuver forward to an imagined destination. But we live this way a lot of the time, and when we do, it is called driving an agenda. There is nothing wrong with applying motivation or aspiration; they are essential for the trip. But focusing entirely on the desired results of our action rather than the action itself makes us a menace to the traveling public and anxious beyond measure.

How many times will you take your feverish child to the doctor to be told, again and again, to ride out the virus, when what you really want to know is how to keep this kid from ever getting sick again?

How exhaustively you might recruit and critique nannies, when what you really want to know is which one you hire today will deliver this child's safety, health, and happiness eighteen years later.

How often will you wonder, "What school should I choose?" when what you really want to know is "What college will it lead to?"

All the knowledge we seek, every question we ask, is the same: "How do I get *there*?" The honest answer to all of them is also the same: "Nobody knows." But do not be afraid. You will always know what you need to know when you need to know it. The truth always reveals itself. The truth reveals itself in a stray cough or a scraped knee, in an unexpected phone call or a conversation overheard. The truth reveals itself in the knock at the door or the accident in the parking lot. It comes in its own costume. The truth reveals itself in an instant of recognition or in a long span of silence. It comes in its own time. We think the truth is found and kept in our heads, when the truth is appearing in front of us all the while. This truth, this ultimate irrefutable truth, is what Buddhists call the Way. The other truth, the truth you try to figure out and manipulate, is called your way. Trying to make things go your way is complicated, harmful, and futile. Things don't always go your way, but they always go. A mother knows best when she learns to simply see how things go and respond accordingly. Living this way is going beyond knowing.

"Do you believe you will get well?" I demanded of my mother, at an early, delusional stage of denial. "I don't know," she said innocently. *Drat!* I thought. *She's not open to the possibilities!* I was wrong. She was open to all the possibilities. I was only open to the one I wanted.

But that's an aside. What you really want to know is how to get your child potty trained. There is a literary subgenre on the topic, and I own a considerable catalog of it. I own the videos and the paperbacks, the children's books and songs. I bought not one but three kinds of potty chairs. I talked with neighbors and nurses. I mused with other moms and concluded the worst: we were behind! Hopelessly, helplessly behind! I gave Georgia the instructions and the edicts. I marked my calendar and set my jaw and tried to make a go of it. We made it go; we just did not make it go in the potty.

In the midst of this, or perhaps because of it, Georgia's seasonal sniffles worsened into a serious infection and she needed high-powered antibiotics. The medicine worked, but its side effect produced such a painful diaper rash that she begged to keep her bottom bare. In an instant, I knew. I pulled the portable potty out and put it by her side that day, the day she potty trained herself.

Learn nothing from this story except to see how things go for you. Do not expect them to go the way they did for me. Do not have any expectations about how things will go. Simply look, listen, wait, and trust. Then, just in time and right on schedule, you'll know for yourself.

These days I steer clear of clusters of moms where anxiety about kids is pandemic. I have my own lingering strain of angst to suppress without spreading it to others.

I read less. For certain, parenting manuals were essential companions in the beginning. At every turn, I needed to know so much. Not long ago I glanced up and saw these books, propping up dust on the shelf of my closet, and realized that many pages and stages had gone unread. So much kindhearted advice had gone unconsulted. It had been years since I sought answers there. No matter, because I remembered the awesome essence of what those books had taught me. Through fevers and rashes, teething and tantrums, those guides had told me to watch and listen, to intuit and discern, to worry less, to wait longer, to trust my child first and to trust myself always.

I only hope I've done as little for you.

26

At Ease

THE GRASS GROWS BY ITSELF

> You naturally arrive at the stage of unaffected ordinariness, which is the ultimate in simplicity and ease. But you never agree to sit there as though dead, falling into the realm of nothingness and unconcern.
>
> —Yuanwu

*S*he can read," my husband said as I carried the grocery sacks into the kitchen.

"She read to me the entire instructions for putting on the belly button tattoo."

I was astonished once again, and not for the reasons you might be. Sure, our moral depravity was advertised all over our daughter's provocatively exposed midriff. But the shocker was that she had just barely slipped out of my belly, out of my arms, off of her trike, and into her fifth year, and she had learned to read. She had learned to read, by my best reckoning, all by herself.

This completed a neat three-peat, a hat trick of amazing feats that she had accomplished with no visible assistance from me.

She had learned to walk, talk, and now, read all by herself. But I'm being too modest on her behalf. From smiling and rolling over to grand jetés and climbing trees, she had done it all without me—and would continue to.

Mothers, it turns out, are not the mothers of invention.

And after all of this hubbub about what to do! What to do now and what to do next, what to do right and what to do better next time. Oh, there is plenty to do, all right—plenty of laundry and plenty of dishes, plenty of caring and loving and fun. Plenty of chatter, babble, and stories; chases, new places, and games. But the real work, the heavy lifting, your child will do by himself. You will wring your hands (preferably when no one is looking), but otherwise your job is to master the delicate art and ineffable substance of doing nothing.

Doing nothing? You think I'm fooling you, and in one sense I am. Doing nothing doesn't quite mean doing nothing. It doesn't mean being lazy, inattentive, or insensitive. It means doing nothing you know you shouldn't be doing. None of the pushing, testing, and prompting we invariably do to get our kids off to the "right start." None of the extra holding, coddling, and protecting we do to keep our babies with us a little longer. It means taking care of what needs to be done right now. And what is that? Whatever is in front of you.

Only from this vantage point does the full marvel of life overcome you—the joy, the freedom, and the simplicity. *You mean, just fill the bathtub?* Yes, the bathtub is the whole of it right now.

I keep a quote from Maria Montessori stuck to the refrigerator door: "Never help a child with a task at which he feels he can succeed." That's half of doing nothing. The other half, attributable to no one, is "Never hurt yourself with the thought that you will fail."

We expect so much of ourselves in this job, and all other tasks before us. Mainly, we expect to really foul it up.

"No one reaches adulthood still drinking milk from a bottle," I was reminded while wandering the wilderness toward full weaning. *My daughter will,* I thought skeptically.

"No child enters kindergarten wearing diapers," I heard often enough. *Here comes the first,* I worried, impatient for the potty.

"Children develop at their own pace," the preschool director gently reproached. "When we grow up, no one ever asks us how old we were when we learned to read." *True,* I conceded, *but am I doing enough to get her started sooner?*

It is difficult to accept the genuine role we have in our children's lives, as it is difficult to accept the genuine role we have in our own lives. It is difficult to be genuine, period. By that I mean even-eyed and open-minded; empty-handed of needles and prods; undistracted by to-dos; never calculating if, when, how, or why. We get our act together only when we let our strategies fall completely apart. Then we can see the inexplicable beauty of the bloom right in front of us.

I will never experience the downhill glide that seems to await mothers on their second or third time around. "This baby is so completely different!" I hear them say. "So easy!" They are completely different mothers too. They are more relaxed and confident. Even in the multiplied chaos they are more at ease, more genuine, and not because they have figured it out but because they have stopped figuring entirely.

My mother was a doer. She was a teacher and a lifelong student. She was a volunteer and a mentor; a church leader and fund-raiser; a doting aunt, attentive sister, cheerful neighbor, eager traveler, letter writer, phone caller, wife, mother, and grandmother. She did all of this all the time in a considerable state of busyness. When she got sick, she stopped doing nearly everything. She stopped planning and managing; she stopped fretting and finally stopped worrying about anyone or anything else. Every day she received a get-well card, or two, or three, for the long stretch of her sickness. She saved them, and toward the end they must have numbered a thousand.

"You are so loved," I marveled, thumbing through the collection.

"And just for being me." She said it softly, humbled at the bounty that befell her even after she let all the doing drop away. She was telling me then what I am telling you now.

You don't have to work so hard at this. You don't have to *do* so much. You don't have to endeavor to be natural, normal, and good. It happens by itself when you least expect it. If you are confused about what you should be doing, try this. *Stop what you are doing.* Take care of what is in front of you, when it is in front of you, and the confusion will pass. This is called the effort of no effort. No effort is what powers the universe.

With time, your roots grow deep and your branches long. You lean a little less backward in fear and a little less forward in doubt, resting solidly right where you are. When the wind blows, you bend. When it stops, you straighten. Your boughs provide shelter and shade. Your strength supports the sky. Sitting quietly, doing nothing, spring comes and the grass grows by itself.

Your baby will be okay.

27

Tending Garden

SEASONS OF MARRIAGE

> Do not be attracted by the sounds of spring or take pleasure in seeing a spring garden. When you see autumn colors, do not be partial to them. You should allow the four seasons to advance in one viewing, and see an ounce and a pound with an equal eye.
>
> —Dogen Zenji, "Instruction for the Tenzo"

> Where there is no romance is the most romantic.
>
> —Hongzhi, "The Truth Body"

They say that your marriage is the garden in which your child grows. Soon enough you will know that it is true, and if you forget, your child will affirm it at every chance. Hope that your garden is a forgiving one, because you may have no interest in gardening for a very long time.

The birth of a child changes everything. It changes everything visibly and invisibly. Of course it must, because it is a powerful and everlasting passage from which there is no return. I survey the aftermath and I see a different me, I hear a different vibration, I quicken to a different impulse. The admonishments sound glib and ridiculous. *Make time for your spouse.* What time is that supposed to be? That blink of time between mere exhaustion and a full-blown mental breakdown?

Yes, that's as good a time as any.

Ultimately, you must return to the route that got you here, to your mate and to your life together as intimates. Perhaps only then does your marriage truly begin—as something other than an idealized romance and your first, naïve coupling as best friends and equals. True friendship takes far longer to cultivate; tested by the shared trauma of parenthood, it may yet flower. But know for a fact that you will no longer be anything approximating equals. That was just an idea. Having a child changes everything.

I am amazed when I see women who seem to have reclaimed their maidenhood after having a child or two or even three. They recapture their looks and rebound into the playful chase of puppy love.

For a long time after giving birth, I was sheathed in loathing and shame over the abdications of my blubbery body. You can be sure that the child you deliver is your own, but the body it comes out of is not. The form that I had spent years sculpting—out of self-devotion, willpower, and free time—was all gone and never again to be beckoned forth. I could not bear my nakedness, and I could scarcely bare my body.

My resentments swelled and crested nearly every day. How unfair the circumstance. How overwhelming the duty. How complete my loneliness as I slogged through the tedium. I could not fault my tiny daughter these offenses; loving her was easy and involuntary. So I faulted my husband. Loving him, you see, was entirely optional. I fortified myself against it with silence and stinginess.

Then there is the job itself: the nearly twenty-four hours of activity and vigilance required by routine child care. We devised an arrangement of time on and time off. We negotiated. We took turns. We each appropriated time away. We talked and fought about it. The tensions were ever present and unspoken: my guilt at being insufficient and his belief that, enabled by his full-time income and supported by his part-time assistance, this was mostly my job to do. Beyond the petty parsing of tasks, I knew that he was right.

This is something that you will know in your marrow, far deeper than social conventions and household roles. Fundamentally and forever, the mother is the mother, and the father is not.

If you're not careful, and we weren't, the *arrangement* becomes the substance of your relationship. That may serve to get you through, but it is not a garden. Everything in it dies.

Onto this tundra comes the purity of angels. If you ever doubted the interdependence of all existence, try gardening. If you ever doubted your child's complete need for an intact family, just listen.

Your child will intuitively and, at first, wordlessly coerce the two of you together at every opportunity. Seeing the two of us together, Georgia coos and glows. She quivers as if to dance. Later, she *will* dance, and she will beam like a delighted grandmother to see us embraced in dance. Once walking, she instructs us emphatically, "Not two. Three!" taking a hand from each of us as she bridges the in-between. One night she directs my husband and me to stand cheek to cheek. "Happy family," she dubs approvingly. Our hearts melt and our eyes lock.

In the dog-eared parenting manual my mother passed on to

me, each of the month-by-month chapters on infant development contains special tips on dealing with divorce. Is this how often the forbidden topic will surface? No, it won't, but it certainly will if your home becomes a hardscrabble no-man's-land.

"We tried to make it work," parents say when they split, shaking their heads and taking off in opposite directions. Oh, you tried to make it *work*? No wonder. Haven't you learned from having a child, haven't you learned from the most joyous, complete, fresh, difficult, undying, robust, intense, demanding relationship in your life that relationships don't *work*? You love your child, and is there anything he or she does that truly *works* for you? That's not what love is. Expect something less from your relationships. Demand something more from yourself.

I have a garden in my backyard. The more time I spend in it, the more beautiful it becomes. Not because of the hard work, the weeding, cleaning, raking, the tasks and sweat, but because I no longer view it as separate from me. From inside the garden, I no longer view it critically from arm's length as flawed, as less than perfect.

You have a garden in your home.

At some point you will wake up, open your heart, turn to your spouse, and do what needs to be done. If your partner is honest and true, you can begin again, on altogether different terms. You will know that good things take time and are sometimes best left undisturbed. You will be more appreciative and kind. You will trust that sunshine follows showers. You will expect less and respect more. You will let things slide and let things go. You will deal quickly with menaces before they choke tender growth. You will say loving things and do loving things and come to know what love means. You will see the seasons of your life in one viewing, each inseparable from the essential sequence. Partial to neither one time nor place, free of idealized notions, you will mature in the romance of no romance. You will be abetted in all of this by your child's sweet adoration of her father and an unbounded need for you both. You will do this because you *can,* and your life is proving to you that you can do anything.

Your life *is* a garden. And you are the only gardener.

28

Beyond Words

THE TIMELESS VOICE OF LOVE

Words! Words!
The Way is beyond language,
for in it there is no yesterday
   no tomorrow
   no today.

—Seng-t'san, "Verses on the Faith-Mind"

I remember her voice, her self-introduction, so needless and formal, on the answering machine. "Karen, this is your mom." I listened quickly, so I wouldn't hear what I was hearing. She sounded weak and small and faraway. How long had she been announcing herself to me that way? All along? Not to disturb, not to impose, not to assume any rank or power in my altogether independent world? Mother to mother, I could recognize something now in the subtle way she stepped back and let go, even on an answering machine. Just love.

The certainty blew through me: this is the last message I'll get. This is her last voice. I didn't want my knowing to invite the fact. I pushed the button, and she disappeared. Disappearing takes only an instant. No, not that long.

My mother died of ovarian cancer after eighteen months of doing her best. We were all doing our best—the doctors and nurses, my family, her friends. She could get better, by the cruelest of margins and for the briefest of interludes, but she could never get over. We used the time and we said the words. We came together and apart, together and apart, and felt under our feet the uncontrollable current that is always propelling life forward.

For months after her diagnosis, when just-born Georgia was still a fuzzy bundle, I loaded the stroller twice a day and patrolled nearby streets looking for a house where my mother could move. I knew it was ridiculous. It was impossible for her to move now, across three states and in the fourth and final stage of cancer. But the need had finally emerged; the understanding had arrived. This is what a mother is for. *To be close by.* Nothing could ever come of it, and it must have been hard for her to hear my silly wishes and fairy-tale dreams knowing that she would have to leave the drama before the end of mine.

Christmas came after her third surgery and before her fourth fruitless round of chemotherapy. No one needed a plan. We all came to her house. When we walked in from the airport she was waiting, shrunken inside a holiday-red turtleneck. Her smile, always ready and big, looked twice its size splayed between sunken cheeks.

Days later, the house nearly empty and quiet, she laid herself down. The crowd had left. Only Georgia and I remained. "I am tired," she said, her only admission, and I watched her wilt like yesterday's balloon. She had been serving us to the end, inflating herself with our needs and expectations. Christmas had been for us, not for her. I gave her then, in my silent acceptance, the only thing she still wanted: permission.

Soon we began to prepare for the after. She told me what she wanted for her funeral, what she wanted for her body, and asked me to write her obituary. I told her that I would never have to live without her. It was a clever comfort spoken without a second thought, the best I could come up with. There would be a few more hurried visits before the long distance would overtake us and I would see for myself if the words were true.

The hospice worker called on a Thursday morning. I was two days home from my mother's bedside. The morphine had arrived and this was good-bye. She put my mother on the line. What to say? "I love you," I said, the words dropping feebly into the thunderous hush of the moment. I heard rustling and whispered conversation. On the other end, there were things to do. All around, there were things to do.

My mother was dying that day. There were things to do. The mundane and ordinary things. The sane and orderly things. Breakfast, lunch. I took Georgia to our music and movement class. We sang and swayed, and the words flooded up. Without knowing, the teacher chose that day to sing this song, giving an accidental touch to an aching heart.

> Who says she'll always come back?
> Your mommy does, that's who.
> Whoever takes care of you comes back
> Because they do love you.

Death is so matter-of-fact. All of this buildup, all of this wild hope and rage, and death comes and goes like the period at the end of a sentence. Once passed, you can't find where it was. *So this is what it means when they say life goes on.* My mother died before the next dawn. I looked around—dazed, awake—taking stock. I had two feet, two hands, two eyes, and an untethered flight ahead of me. Of course I grieved; of course I cried. Looking up, there was life, the full laundry basket of life, going on.

Perhaps all traditions are oral traditions. My mother's voice has never left me. Her love has never left me. I feel her absence but never her loss. I hear her reassurance and her laughter. I see in my eyes and my aging grace a face that grows only more familiar. I am my mother. No other.

In the cozy darkness a year later, tucking in my three-year-old, I ask her what she loves best. "Your voice," she says, dreamily. She is halfway dreaming, when answers are undefiled. I am reassured. It will change a bit, weaken and grow old. And then she will hear it in herself: a song without words, a lyric beyond language, a smile, a laugh, a moment's silent consolation. It will always come back because it never leaves. I know that voice.

29

Why Not

NO RIGHT ANSWERS,
ONLY A RIGHT QUESTION

Students should know that the Buddha Way lies outside thinking, analysis, prophesy, introspection, knowledge and wise explanation.

—Dogen Zenji, "Guidelines for Studying the Way"

*L*ong ago I sat at a table filled with someone else's relatives at a wedding reception for a couple I hardly knew. This was during the taut time of my first, childless marriage. Amid the risqué toasts and familiar jokes, a long-fingered grandmother pointed to me, a stranger. "Why not children?" she probed, with old-country audacity. "You have no children, you have fear of life."

Why not children? Why not life? Why not?

She was rude but she was right. Nearly twenty years later I would finally risk asking myself the same question. You may not have an explanation for starting your family; perhaps, like me, you just dropped the reasons not to. Dropping reasons is a good habit to get into.

Like the road that got you here, the road through parenthood is unmarked. You can't cruise through it. Sometimes decisions are quick and instinctual, but often they're not. Doubts and dilemmas block every straightaway. There's only one directional sign along the way, and it reads, "Why not?"

If there's one question I wish I asked myself more often, one question that I vow to ask faster, it's this one. It saves so much time and energy. It opens doors and solves problems. It eases everyone's growth and change. And it makes things interesting because it leads where you have never been before.

Never place your child in the care of another? Why not let others love them too?

Never manage without a nanny? Why not try it yourself?

Never consider quitting work? Why not sacrifice money for love?

Never going back to work? Why not introduce your child to the rest of you?

Never spent the night away from your child? Why not prove that you always come back?

Never give up your night out? Why not forgo the movies for a while?

Never have your child immunized? Why not believe what doctors say?

Never doubt your pediatrician? Why not listen to your instincts?

Never have chocolate pudding for breakfast? Why not have fun today?

Never have time to cook a homemade meal? Why not start right now?

Never have another child? Why not appreciate what comes?
Never have an only child? Why not accept things as they are?

I'm not suggesting that you be cavalier about the serious issues before you, or careless about your child's health and security.
I am warning you that as soon as you arrive at an ironclad ration-
ale about anything, the target practice will begin. Slings, arrows,
potshots, splattered tomatoes, and pies in the face. *Here's that question coming at you again. See how you handle it this time.*

So much gobbledygook is our own making. We tangle ourselves in convoluted reasoning, bog ourselves in doubt, bury
ourselves in fear, and then we complain about the working
conditions.

One morning in June of her third year, Georgia woke up
and asked, "Is it summer?" When I told her yes, she shot upright,
"Do I have swimming lessons today?" I jerked alert to the unmistakable screech of a window opening, the knock of opportunity arriving, and I knew what I would do. We signed up for
swimming lessons.

But several days into her first week's tutorial, she woke up
and said something else. She said, "I don't feel well." I could tell
she wasn't sick, and we had five minutes to get to the pool.

"Don't you want to go to your swimming lesson?" I asked.

"I want to stay in my bed."

"Did something happen?" I implored.

"No, Momma."

I was flummoxed. Then she gestured for me to come close.

"I have a secret," she whispered, cupping my ear. "I'm afraid
my teacher will let go of me."

Oh, my poor sweet girl.

"Okay," I improvised, "Let's go tell her. Let's go tell her not
to let go of you."

She bounded out of bed and popped into her suit. We hurried to the pool, and she ran up to her teacher.

"Please don't let go of me!" she burst out, beaming with relief. Her teacher wisely agreed. Freed from the secret bondage of fear, she went back into the water, and she learned to swim.

It wasn't that this was easy for her. She worked hard and overcame her self-doubt. It wasn't that this objective was imposed on her; it came from an unwavering source within. I was awed by her heroic advance. She was learning to swim. And why not, I asked myself, why not?

I jerked alert to the unmistakable screech of a window opening, and I knew what I would do. Even as I was admiring her baby strokes, I had been nursing my own secret fear. I, too, was afraid of the water. Another kind of water.

One morning soon after I saw Georgia take her plunge—afraid yet emboldened, uncertain yet unstoppable—I told my Zen teacher, "I will ordain." And why not? The reasons had popped like so many bubbles before you finally come up for air.

I had been holding myself back from my Zen practice: making excuses for going only so far, rationalizing my fear into self-decreed shortages of time and commitment. I had called myself a Zen Buddhist for nearly ten years, and I pursued my practice regularly. But I was a wife, I told myself. I was a wife and mother for goodness' sake. I was a wife and mother and I had things to do first and places to go after that! Holding tight to the side of the pool, secure in my comfort zone, how far would I swim into the deep end of this Buddhist thing?

There are many things you *can* do in life, but the things that you accomplish are those to which you commit. This is true of all things, and some of them are very important things, like marriage, motherhood, and a spiritual practice. This commitment may be public, or it may be deeply private, but you always know the promises you have made. In a Zen practice, there are several opportunities to make a commitment to yourself. The first is when you choose a teacher and commit to being a student. Your personal commitment is formalized in a public ceremony at which you take vows defining how you intend to live as a Buddhist. For example, you vow not to kill, lie, or steal, or be angry, boastful, critical, stingy, hurtful, and the like. The next opportunity—though not chosen by everyone, and never required of anyone—is to take the vows of priesthood. This is when you vow to do all of the above *forever*. When you take this vow, you receive exquisite flowing robes. And you lose all the hair on your head.

How can I explain the sudden realization? I can't. How can I rationalize it? I won't. And I won't make light of it: shaving my head was a very big phobia. Sure, I understood it. It symbolizes a conscious parting from the entangling ego, a mighty blow to the phantasm of self-image. But it petrified me; it paralyzed me. Then in one moment, the moment of my utterance, the obstacle became very small. Suddenly—poof!—it was gone. Hair is like that.

People ask me what it means to be a priest. That is a good question that I must answer by my actions every moment of my life, because I have taken a vow. Does a silly little vow make a difference? Not for everyone, all the time. For instance, there are people who live together, unmarried, and say, "How could a vow make a difference?" (I've done that too.) And then you make a vow and you find that it makes *all the difference*. Being a priest means that I have committed myself to a lifetime of service, but this is not some special kind of service that is dolloped on top of the life I already have. I serve my family, I serve my home, I serve my friends, I serve everyone and everything I encounter. I serve them by being selfless. Is this such a big promise? Considering that otherwise my only inclination would be to serve myself, yes, it is a big promise.

In Buddhism, priests are called "home leavers." People naturally wonder if this means abandoning my family to take up a life of solitude, study, or ceremony elsewhere. But whom would that serve? I tell them that my family's home is not the home that I have vowed to leave. I promised to leave my ego's home, that nest of selfish desires and provocations, where all of my problems start, simmer, and spill over, where the malcontent shrieks in eternal frustration, "Me! Me! Me!" Every day I make the bed in this home, tidy up, turn out the lights, and walk away. Only then can I make the beds, tidy up, and get to work in the Miller house doing what needs to be done.

You might say that sounds like the life of a mother. You are so right. In my home, the life of a priest, a wife, and a mother are one and the same. I have only one life and my life is only one thing. Motherhood doesn't get in the way of being a priest, and being a priest doesn't get in the way of being a mother. My practice is to see that nothing ever gets in the way of anything else. More to the point, my practice is to recognize that no one else is ever pushing me forward, and no one else is ever holding me back.

Georgia jumped in and learned to swim like a mermaid that summer. She learned to stand on her hands underwater. She never lost another minute to hesitation. I became a Zen Buddhist priest that fall. I learned that I could leave home and lose nothing, nothing at all. (Hair grows back, and I keep it short to remind myself that I have nothing to lose.)

Our lives, our circumstances, and our choices are uniquely our own. There are no right answers. But there *is* a right question. It's the one that rubs up against our self-righteousness, re-sistance, and fears. The one that revolves a *never* into a *maybe* into an *okay, let's see.* When you ask yourself, "Why not?" you may find that you are no longer stepping reflexively backward or standing rigidly still. You could instead find yourself in motion, across a vivid and unpredictable landscape, over impossible mountains and beyond the deep blue water's edge, where you surprise your-self, once and for all, by getting wet.

30

Happily After

A WISE MOTHER'S INHERITANCE

> Ummon addressed the assembly and said, "I am not asking
> you about the days before the fifteenth of the month. But
> what about after the fifteenth? Come and give me a word
> about those days." And he himself gave the answer for them:
> "Every day is a good day."
>
> —*Blue Cliff Record*, case 6

*T*here comes a day in the life of a child when he or she
exits the confines of the world you have so intelligently
chosen and resurfaces in a world of his or her own. When this
happens you might cringe and resist, bemoan and protest. You
probably had your own game plan for firing up your child's
synapses. You intended to have the final say in what she loved
most of all and wore four straight days and nights without washing. You were going to steer clear of all plastic and crassness, for
starters, and never utter the words *french* and *fry* in succession. All
for naught. Now your child loves nothing else, plays with noth-

ing else, wears nothing else, and demands nothing other than your own worst fears.

When this happens, step lightly and listen up. In your child's devotions, the gods may have a message for you. They did for me.

Late in her second year, Georgia went to the mall in a pair of sensible Stride-Rites and overalls. She came home in a blue ball gown and cheap heels. She had entered a new universe, the Magic Kingdom of the world's second-largest media conglomerate. She had arrived at her princess years. Instantly our household was transformed into a churning cog in the greater scheme to maximize earnings and cash flow and allocate capital profitably toward growth initiatives that will drive long-term shareholder value. That is to say, we bought a lot of stuff. We bought a lot of stuff for the princess that wears blue, then the one in pink, then yellow, then the princess with the falsetto voice and seven short roommates. We dabbled in smaller collections for the redhaired princess with fins and the tiny lime green fairy with wings. We were caught in a vortex of discovery, passion, delight, and the desperate need to prevent tantrums in public places.

Being the mom described in this chapter's first paragraph, I decided to piggyback on this obsession and score at least a few stray points in the reading category. I bought the full suite of princess read-aloud storybooks. Bedtimes were given over to endless recitations of "once upon a time" and "happily ever after," with an assortment of entirely inappropriate crimes and misdemeanors in between. Reading these stories was itself an athletic exercise—leaping over words like *evil, hate,* and *kill* without losing the beat, eliminating whole scenes without skipping a page.

Still, they were happily-ever-after stories, one after the other after the other, and most days I was anything but. I was not, for the greater measure, living happily at all.

A few hundred readings of this stuff and it might get through to you. Finally it did to me. I had sat in the same rocking chair, reading the same books, for bedtimes upon bedtimes, and one night I realized where I was. *I* was the one with the book in my hand. *I* was the one hearing the words. *I* had, indeed, one day found a prince; *I* was the one who had fallen in love; *I* was the one with the fairy-tale wedding; *I* was the one at home in a castle; *I* was the princess, wasn't I now, with a junior princess on my lap? Do you think this message could possibly be for me? Could *I* give a go at living happily? I know it's just make-believe, but who makes it real? *I* could, by being happy.

That's a mighty leap, you could say, to extract the sublime from the ridiculous. But it was true for me. It was a bull's-eye hit. I was unhappy a lot of the time. When I wasn't, I might be annoyed or impatient and intermittently resentful. This was obvious to everyone. My daughter could read between my furrows and inflections. She would break my troubled silences with a stunningly simple question, "Momma, are you happy now?"

Gasp. And from the mouth of a two-year-old.

Happy now? Yes, I would snap awake, realizing in that moment that I could choose and change, and by changing my attitude, change everything. Being happy is worth everything. It is my heart's desire. Isn't it every heart's desire? It's what I want most for my child. Being healthy is great, kind is sweet, smart is convenient, but happy matters most of all.

Happy matters most of all. And here's the surprise ending. You don't have to wait for happiness, because there's no time but now to be happy. You don't have to go somewhere else, because there's no place but here to find it. You don't have to do something else, because there's nothing more to it. You don't have to get something else, because everything you already have is enough. You just have to be happy.

Is it really that simple? Yes. Is it really that easy? No. That's how we all arrived on this page.

And yet there is such a thing as happiness. There is such a place as bliss. When you drop your expectations, lose your selfishness, forget your grievances, give up your worries, abandon the plan, stop your striving, let it out, let it go, let things pass, take a breath, take a break, quiet down, be still, empty your mind, open your heart, and come alive, what else is there to be but happy? If you can answer otherwise, it's time to read this paragraph again and see what you've overlooked.

My mother had been happy. It was how I would always remember her. "She was so happy," I said in her eulogy. "It drew people to her, to her comfort and ease." Hers was a life with so many more aches and breaks than mine. So many hardships, so little gained. There was hardly a reason for her to be happy, but I remember her first, last, and most as happy. Now I wonder. Perhaps she had been happy as a gift to me, to a child that wants and needs and loves a happy mother above all else. Happy is the sign that all is well and will be. It is the seed of faith, optimism, and commitment. It is such fertile ground. Everything thrives there.

The last time I saw my mother, she sat upright in her bed and took me in without flinching. "I guess it's time to say good-bye," she said. "Be yourself and take good care of your family." I swallowed hard and nodded my farewell.

It was a prescription for happiness; it was my inheritance. Taking good care of your family is no different from taking good care of yourself. There is nothing more gratifying. There is nothing more immediate. There is nothing more available. Every day is a good day to take care. Every moment. This moment.

Master Hongzhi wrote, "The house of silent illumination is the hall of pure bliss." The house is yours. The hall is you. It can sound trifling, but attaining pure bliss is no mere trivial pursuit. It is no pursuit at all, because it is already abiding within you.

We think bliss magically arrives or mysteriously eludes. *Perhaps it will come after the fifteenth?* But happiness is, all along, in abundant supply within us. We can survive the wicked witches, the fire-breathing dragons, and all of our dire imaginings. We can escape the locked dungeons, unscalable towers, imprisoning judgments, and self-limiting fears. We can outlast the poisons, curses, misfortunes, and unforeseen perils. We simply have to be what, in our silent depths, we already are. We simply have to do what, in our inexplicable wisdom, we can do without a second thought.

This is your new spiritual practice: cracking a smile.

Queens and princesses, storytellers and teachers, wise women and sages, had given me final instructions. Here in my own house, in my own rocking chair, with my baby curled close and held fast, I had heard them at last. All of it, every bit of it, comes down to this:

May we all live happily ever after.

HOW TO MEDITATE
Finding a moment in the midst

> Practicing Zen is zazen. For zazen a quiet place is suitable.
> Set aside all involvements and let the myriad things rest.
>
> —Dogen Zenji, "Rules for Zazen"

Finding calm in the midst of fury, finding inspiration in the midst of despair, finding strawberry jam sandwiched between the sofa cushions, finding the splinter betwixt two tender toes. Moms can find anything in a pinch, except a moment for themselves.

Meditation is the best way to find that moment. It is the best way to find *any* moment, and telling you how to meditate is the only lasting good that I can give you. A regular (or irregular!) meditation practice will give you more of the focus and discipline you need to do everything else: listen, talk, teach, comfort, work, play, relax, go to sleep, wake up, and do it all over again. It's a little bit of attention paid to yourself so you can give all the rest of your attention away.

If you're like me, you might say you can't possibly find the time to meditate. Until one day you do. Here's how to proceed when that day arrives.

To start, let go of the ideas you may have about what meditation is supposed to look like or what it is supposed to feel like.

Unless you have a meditation cushion, or zafu, do not attempt to sit cross-legged on the floor to meditate. Without adequate support to elevate your buttocks and enable you to anchor your knees on the floor, sitting this way quickly becomes painful. The point of meditation is not pain. Your life is painful enough as it is. The point of meditation is to relieve pain.

What follows are instructions for meditating in a chair. Although you are unlikely to have the perfect chair in your home for meditation, any chair is perfectly okay.

1. Sit on the forward third of a chair so that your feet rest firmly on the ground. To support your back, place a hard cushion between your spine and the chair back. This will prevent slouching and keep you alert.

2. Space your feet widely apart. Your body is now supported at three points: your two feet and your bottom. In seated meditation, three contact points are essential for endurance and comfort. Your body now evokes the strength of a mountain.

3. Place your hands in the middle of your lap as follows: first your right hand, palm up; then your left hand, palm up, resting in your right palm. Lightly touch the tips of your thumbs together. Holding your hands in this way calms agitation and restlessness.

4. To check your posture, align your ears with your shoulders. Align your nose with your navel. Tuck your chin in slightly. Hold your head as though it were supporting the sky and it will neither hang forward nor fall backward.

5. Relax your belly. A stiff, cinched abdomen restricts your breathing. In meditation, you will try to return to the full, rounded breathing of a baby. Watch your baby breathe and see that it is the belly that rises on inhalation, not the chest. This is a good observation for you to learn from.

6. Lower your gaze, but do not close your eyes. If you close your eyes, you will be lulled into daydreaming. Meditation is not practice for sleeping; it is practice for waking up. Look at a spot on the floor or on a wall in front of you. Any spot will do, as long as it is not distracting.

7. Close your teeth and your mouth. Take a breath and exhale completely.

8. On your next inhalation, silently count "one." When you exhale, silently count "two."

Inhale counting "three." Count each exhalation and inhalation up to ten and then start back at one. If you lose the count, begin again at one. This meditation practice is called counting your breath.

9. When a thought comes up, let it go away by itself, which it will if you do not pursue it.

10. This is the practice of zazen. Do zazen for up to five minutes. Keep a watch or clock nearby to note the time. As you meditate more often, you may be able to do it for longer. Do not be self-critical or impatient with yourself. Do not push yourself. Do not make meditation one more thing you have to do. If you are gentle, encouraging, and consistent with yourself, your meditation practice will naturally deepen and lengthen.

Five minutes is not a long time, but it can take a long time to find five minutes to meditate. Usually the first five minutes or the last five minutes in the day are the easiest to find. You already have them and they are already quiet.

FOR THE HARD DAYS
Where to look for help

This book is full of help, but no one needs help with the happy times. When you don't have the luxury of a long pause, take these shortcuts for the reassurance to calm the crisis of the day.

WHEN YOU NEED A LITTLE	SEE CHAPTER
Balance	11 or 17
Break	11, 15, 21, or 26
Confidence	4, 20, or 25
Courage	3, 14, 21, 25, or 29
Creativity	6, 9, or 23
Discipline	12, 13, or 18
Encouragement	7, 25, 26, or 29
Endurance	8 or 15
Forgiveness	7, 14, 18, or 19
Fun	15, 23, or 24
Laughter	13, 15, 16, 17, or 30
Love	2, 20, 27, or 28

For the Hard Days

CREDITS

The author is grateful to the following translators, editors, and publishers for permission to use passages from these classic works of Zen literature:

Excerpts from *Moon in a Dewdrop* by Dogen, translated by Kazuaki Tanahashi. Translation copyright © 1985 by the San Francisco Zen Center. Reprinted by permission of North Point Press, a division of Farrar, Straus and Giroux, LLC.

Koan cases of *The Gateless Gate* and *The Blue Cliff Record* from *Two Zen Classics,* translated with commentaries by Katsuki Sekida, edited by A.V. Grimstone. Copyright © 1977 by Katsuki Sekida and A.V. Grimstone. Reprinted by arrangement with Weatherhill, an imprint of Shambhala Publications, Inc., Boston, www.shambhala.com.

Seng-t'san, excerpts from *Hsin-Hsin Ming: Verses on the Faith-Mind,* translated by Richard B. Clarke. Copyright © 1973, 1984, 2001 by Richard B. Clark. Reprinted with the permission of White Pine Press, Buffalo, New York, www.whitepine.org.

Yuanwu, excerpts from *Zen Letters,* translated by J. C. Cleary and Thomas Cleary. Copyright © 1994. Reprinted by arrangement with Shambhala Publications, Inc., Boston, www.shambhala.com.

Hongzhi, excerpts from *Cultivating the Empty Field: The Silent Illumination of Zen Master Hongzhi,* translated by Taigen Dan Leighton with Yi Wu, edited by Taigen Dan Leighton. Copyright © 2000 by Dan Leighton. Reprinted by permission of Tuttle Publishing of Boston and Tokyo.

Karen Maezen Miller is a mother, wife, writer, and Zen Buddhist priest. After a twenty-year career in public relations, she backed unsuspectingly into midlife motherhood, which she soon realized presented her with nonstop, real-life spiritual practice. Miller began her Zen study with Taizan Maezumi Roshi, one of the first Japanese masters to bring Zen to the West. Following

Maezumi Roshi's death in 1995, the author continued training under his successor, Nyogen Yeo Roshi, the abbot of Hazy Moon Zen Center of Los Angeles, where she is now a dharma holder and meditation instructor. She and her family live in Sierra Madre, California, amid a ninety-year-old Japanese garden.

For more information or to contact the author, visit www.mommazen.com.